THE CHOICE OF THE PEOPLE?

Enduring Questions in American Political Life
Series Editor: Wilson Carey McWilliams, Rutgers University

This series explores the political, social, and cultural issues that originated during the founding of the American nation but are still heatedly debated today. Each book offers teachers and students a concise but comprehensive summary of the issue's evolution, along with the crucial documents spanning the range of American history. In addition, *Enduring Questions in American Political Life* provides insightful contemporary perspectives that illuminate the enduring relevance and future prospects of important issues on the American political landscape.

The Choice of the People? Debating the Electoral College
Judith A. Best, introduction by Thomas E. Cronin

Debating the Role of Religion in Public Life
Ted Jelen and Mary Segers, introduction by Clarke E. Cochran

THE CHOICE OF THE PEOPLE?

Debating the Electoral College

Judith A. Best

Foreword by
Thomas E. Cronin

ROWMAN & LITTLEFIELD PUBLISHERS, INC.

ROWMAN & LITTLEFIELD PUBLISHERS, INC.

Published in the United States of America
by Rowman & Littlefield Publishers, Inc.
4720 Boston Way, Lanham, Maryland 20706

3 Henrietta Street
London WC2E 8LU, England

British Cataloging in Publication Information Available

Library of Congress Cataloging-in-Publication Data

Best, Judith.
The choice of the people? : debating the electoral college / by
Judith A. Best.
p. cm.
Includes bibliographical references and index.
1. Electoral college—United States. 2. Presidents—United
States—Election. I. Title. JK529.B45 1996 324.6'0973—dc20 96-
572 CIP

ISBN 0–8476–8216–1 (cloth : alk. paper)
ISBN 0–8476–8217–x (pbk. : alk. paper)

Printed in the United States of America

∞ ™ The paper used in this publication meets the minimum requirements of
American National Standard for Information Sciences—Permanence of
Paper for Printed Library Materials, ANSI Z39.48–1984.

Contents

v

vi   *Contents*

Foreword
The Electoral College Controversy

Thomas E. Cronin

The American electoral college is a deplorable political institution. . . . If the electoral college were only a neutral and sure means for counting and aggregating votes, it would be the subject of little controversy. The electoral college, however, is neither certain in its operations nor neutral in its effects. . . . In short, the electoral college is a flawed means of determining the president. Its workings at best are neither smooth nor fair, and at worst contain the potential for constitutional crisis. . . . It must be abolished.

—Lawrence D. Longley

A constitution is not simply the highest and most solemn law a people can make, it is an organic arrangement of interdependent balanced parts. It is like a solar system where the entire system is dependent upon each planet being in its place, each moving in its own orbit around the sun, and if you change a part, you change the whole. . . . The electoral vote system in presidential elections not only is part of this constitutional solar system, it is the . . . very model of our democratic federal republic. . . .

—Judith A. Best

The electoral college system for the election of American presidents was much debated at the Constitutional Convention of 1787 and since then it has been about the most widely debated aspect in the Constitution. "Over the years," writes one historian, "no other provision has drawn so much criticism or provoked so many constitutional amendments as has the electoral college clause."[1] There have probably been close to a thousand proposed constitutional amendments aimed at fixing or abolishing this process. Congress on several occasions has held highly publicized hearings on electoral college reform.

The typical American does not usually claim to understand much about the electoral college, its origins, or its consequences. Still, pollsters regularly report their polls indicate that majorities of adult Americans would dump the electoral college "system" in favor of a direct one-person-one-vote system to elect American presidents. People wonder, too, why such an antique system still exists in the cyberspace age and question whether a better way can't be found to select presidents.

Political writers and commentators grumble a lot about the electoral college and its problems. They do so largely because this system does not assure victory to the presidential candidate who wins a majority of the popular vote. And we have had some notably close elections. The election of 1960, for example, was won by one-tenth of 1 percent of the popular vote. Kennedy won several states by less than 1 or 2 percent of the popular vote in each, and these states had more than enough electoral votes to win or lose the election for him.

Yet political reform of the electoral college has not made much progress in recent years. The road to electoral college reform is littered with the wrecks of dozens of previous efforts. Part of the problem is that while some of the ills or undesirable side effects of the electoral college are clear, no one is wholly clear about what the consequences would be if we abolished the electoral college and substituted in its stead some other election procedures.

Political scientists and informed commentators are notably divided over whether to retain the electoral college. Some hail America's system for electing an executive as "the most successful in the world" and as "an antique that works."[2] Other scholars say the electoral college system has worked well enough despite its flaws, and they like to quote the old saw, "if it ain't broke, don't fix it."

But many scholars hold the view that our system of selecting presidents is a constitutional accident waiting to happen. One day we will end up with a clear loser in the White House, they say. "And the question is, will this loser/winner be seen as legitimate at home and abroad? If 'we the people' would amend the Constitution *after* the loser President materializes . . . why are we now just waiting for the inevitable accident to happen?'' [3]

What Did the Founders Intend?

The framers agonized over how to devise a system for electing the president. They considered election by Congress at least four times but rejected it. Election by the people was voted down twice. The delegates disliked the idea of election by Congress because this would have made presidents too dependent on the national legislature, especially if they wanted to run for reelection. They were even more opposed to direct election by the people because many delegates thought it unlikely or impractical for the average citizen to know enough about candidates from other states, and doubtless, too, most delegates questioned the ability of the people to cast responsible votes.

There was another highly political reason why many of the delegates sought some system other than election directly by the voters. If a system of direct election by the people had been adopted, the slave states like Virginia and North Carolina would stand to lose the advantage they enjoyed in what the convention had approved for the House of Representatives. Under direct popular voting, only the enfranchised white population could vote; whereas, if the Congress did the voting, the added clout of the Southern states, whose slaves counted as three-fifths of one person for purposes of representation, would be lost.

In the end, the electoral college the framers devised was a special, temporary congress elected to select a president, but without the shortcoming of relying on the regular Congress. Any fear of plotting or corruption was allayed by the fact that delegates would meet in their respective states.

The electoral college, as devised by the constitutional framers, was neither a deliberate exercise in denying voters the right to vote for president nor a product of some grand concept of political theory. Rather, "The delegates were confronted with a practical problem arising from the constellation of clashing forces at Philadelphia, and they devised a practical solution—an ad hoc congress that would faithfully reflect the patterns of weighted voting that was an integral part of the operation of the real Congress.''[4] The framers offered the electoral college as an artful compromise between the small and large states, between North and South, and between the proponents of a decentralized federal republic and those who favored a stronger national government. And they wanted to protect the independence of the office, especially from Congress.

Simply put, the nation was to have electors in each of the states—equal in number to a state's delegation to Congress—choose the president. A majority of the electors' votes would be required for election.

It was an ingenious and original compromise. Everyone got something: large states got electoral votes based on their population; small states got an assurance of at least three electoral votes and a contingency procedure based on a one-state-one vote principle. Those who feared a "tyranny of the majority" got an indirect method of electing presidents. Those who feared the national legislature got a method in which the states could play a major role. Those in the slave states got a counting method that factored in added voting strength to reflect their slave population.

Alexander Hamilton, writing in the Federalist essays, praised the compromise and noted that the people in the states in one way or another would help choose the electors and then the electors would choose the president. Yet he seemed especially impressed that the immediate election would be made by a small, capable, and judicious elite who would be most likely to possess the discernment and information required to make such an important decision.

Others believed, and perhaps hoped, that once George Washington had completed his term or possibly several terms, the electors under this process would fail to produce majorities and thus the president would be chosen by contingency means in the House of Representatives. Convention delegate George Mason from Virginia thought presidential selection would be made in the House nineteen out of twenty times.

Plainly, as compromises go, it was a gamble. Plainly, too, the American political system and party politics in America have significantly changed since 1787.

How It Works Today

The framers might be amazed to find the electoral college still in operation. It was a compromise and perhaps even an improvisation that has over the years taken on the aura of a political monument. Yet it is a controversial, criticized, and poorly understood monument.

A lot has changed since 1787. Political parties came into existence and have for a long while organized much of our participation in elections. There has been a considerable nationalization of American politics. There has also developed in America a pretty strong conviction that everyone should have an equal voice and thus an equal vote in the elections of mayors, governors, U.S. representatives, and presidents. The suffrage has been greatly extended. High voter turnout is considered valuable. Also, faith in the people is greater than it was in the 1780s.

Many of the framers expected electors to be designated by state legislatures. The electors, as noted above, would be distinguished citizens who would, in fact as well as in form, nominate and then elect a president and a vice president. The rise of national political parties changed all this. By the election of 1800, electors by custom had become party agents, usually pledged in advance to vote for designated party candidates.

How does the system work today? In making their presidential choice in November, voters technically do not vote for a candidate but choose between slates of presidential electors selected by state political parties. Except in Maine and Nebraska, the slate that wins a plurality of popular votes in the state casts all the electoral votes for that state. A state has one electoral vote for each senator and each representative. The District of Columbia has three votes, granted to it by the Twenty-third Amendment. There are 538 votes in the electoral college today. A presidential candidate must get 270 or more to win.

Technically, a president is not elected on election day. Citizens do not technically vote for candidates either, but for electors. Victorious slates of electors travel to their state capitols on the first Monday after the second Wednesday in December, where they cast ballots for their party's candidates. Ballots are sent from the state capitals to Congress, where early in January they are formally counted by House and Senate leaders and the next president is finally announced.

If no candidate secures a majority of electoral votes, the decision then goes to the House of Representatives. This has happened twice, once in 1800 and again in 1824. People feared it might happen again in 1968 when George Wallace ran, or in 1992 when H. Ross Perot ran a strong independent campaign. In the House, each delegation casts a single vote. If a delegation is evenly divided, the state forfeits its vote. The influence of a third-party "spoiler" candidate may be significant, because the House chooses a president from among the top three candidates. Consecutive ballots are taken until a candidate wins a majority (twenty-six) of the state delegations.

Complaints of Those Who Favor the Direct Election of Presidents

The direct election method means the person who gets the most votes wins. There is no electoral college. Advocates of the direct popular system contend everyone's vote should count equally, people should vote directly for the candidate, and the candidate who gets the majority of votes should be elected.

With the electoral college method, a president can be elected who has fewer popular votes than his opponent, as was the case in 1824 when John Quincy Adams, with 30.92 percent of the vote, defeated Andrew Jackson with 41.34 percent of the vote. This happened again in 1876 when Rutherford Hayes, with 47.95 percent of the popular vote, won over Tilden with 50.97 percent of the vote; and in 1888, when Benjamin Harrison won the presidency with 47.82 percent over Grover Cleveland with 48.62 percent. This can happen because all of a state's electoral votes are awarded to the winner of the state's popular vote regardless of whether the winning candidate's margin is one vote or three million votes.

Ironically, the major "defect" here, the unit-rule provision, is not part of the Constitution. This winner-take-all formula (unit rule) is merely a state practice, first adopted in the early nineteenth century for partisan purposes, and gradually accepted by the rest of the states to ensure maximum electoral weight for their state in the national election. In recent years, Maine and Nebraska have modified the winner-take-all allocation rule. In these states, two electoral votes go to the statewide plurality winner and one vote goes to each plurality victor in each of the state's House of Representative's congressional districts.

But because the rest of the states use this rule, the electoral college benefits large "swing" states at the expense of the middle-sized states. The winner-take-all arrangement in the states magnifies the relative power of residents in large states. As political scientist Larry Longley suggests, each of the voters in the ten largest states might, by their vote, "decide not just one popular vote, but how a bloc of 33 to 54 votes are cast—if electors are faithful." Hence, the electoral college has a major impact on candidate strategy. Most recent presidential candidates have spent much of their time in the closing weeks of the campaign in crucial states such as California, Illinois, Michigan, Ohio, Pennsylvania, and New York.[5]

The smaller states are advantaged by the "constant two" electoral votes. Thus, Alaska may get 1 electoral vote for every 40,000 popular votes, whereas Minnesota may get 1 for every 200,000 popular votes. In the 1990s, "the seven states with 3 electoral votes each had a ratio of 268,000 or fewer citizens per electoral vote, while every state with 13 or more electoral votes had a ratio of 475,000 or more citizens per electoral vote."[6]

In contrast to the complexities and dangers of the electoral college system, the direct-vote method is appealing in its simplicity. Since it is based on a one-person-one-vote principle, it more clearly makes a president the agent of the people and not of the states. Governors and senators are elected by statewide direct popular voting, and they are supposed to be agents of the state. The president, however, should be president of the people, not president of the states—or at least this is what reformers say.

Most of those who favor a direct popular election of president base their views on the undemocratic character of the electoral college. They say it doesn't treat voters equally, it discourages turnout, and it discriminates against third parties and independent presidential candidates. They point out that those living in large states and small states get more influence. They point out that Democrats in Kansas or Idaho and Republicans in the District of Columbia are usually discouraged from even turning out to vote since votes are cast in bloc and the chances of their party winning are small.

Critics also rightly complain that, in most instances, voters are wasting their vote if they vote for a John Anderson or Ross Perot or a Green Party candidate for the White House. The winner-take-all simply invites a voter to steer clear of minor or new parties, to avoid wasting their vote. They are, in effect, greatly discouraged from considering anyone other than the Democrat or the Republican.

Thus, there are major questions of fairness and democracy that constantly get raised in the debate over the electoral college and its alternatives. A direct popular vote would eliminate undesirable and undemocratic biases. Writes Stephen J. Wayne:

> It would better equalize voting power both among and within states. . . . The large, competitive states would lose some of their electoral clout by the elimination of winner-take-all voting. Party competition within the states and perhaps nationwide would be increased. Candidates would be forced to wage campaigns in all fifty states. No longer could an area of the country be taken for granted. Every vote would count in a direct election.[7]

Critics of the electoral college system invariably also attack the contingency election procedure and would change the contingency procedure to a popular run-off. The current system provides that if no presidential candidate wins an absolute majority of the electoral votes (270 under present arrangements), the members of the House of Representatives choose a president from the top three vote getters. The members vote as a part of their state delegation with each state having just one vote. Thus, both Alaska and California have one vote, both Delaware and New York get just one vote, and both Wyoming and Texas get one vote.

If this contingency procedure had to be used in future elections, it would obviously be a big boon for small states. But more important, critics lament, it would be an incredibly undemocratic way to select a president. Further, the intrigues in the House might prove unseemly, especially in a three-person, three-party race.

The direct-vote plan would do away with the present electors who occasionally have voted for persons who did not win the plurality vote in their states. This is the so-called faithless elector problem. Since our first election, fewer than a dozen electors have been faithless among more than twenty thousand. These few miscast votes have never made a difference. Still, the process seems anachronistic and potentially dangerous. There are virtually no defenders of this aspect of the electoral college.

Thus, proponents of the direct vote say it is the most forthright alternative and far preferable to the present system. They contend that voters, when they are choosing a president, think of themselves as national citizens, not as residents of a particular state. In the words of the American Bar Association, the present system is "archaic, undemocratic, complex, ambiguous, indirect and dangerous."[8] The direct popular vote system, on the other hand, proponents claim, is simple, democratic, and clear cut.

Why Proponents Favor Retaining the Electoral College

Those who favor retaining the electoral college usually argue their case with passion. They emphasize the wisdom of the founders and stress that ours is a federal system, not a unified, centralized, pure hierarchical nationalized system. They remind us that our nation was founded as a republic with a number of checks and balances.

Plainly the founders designed the electoral college in part to modify or check the probability that popular majorities might choose the wrong person for president. Nowadays, the principal effect of the electoral college is to give added weight to the large, highly populated, and typically industrial states, offsetting in part the greater clout of the smaller and more rural states in Congress.

Advocates for retaining the electoral college contend we should not lightly dismiss a system that has served us so well for so long. One constitutional scholar wrote:

> We are well served by an attachment to institutions that are often the products more of accident than of design, or that no longer answer to their original purposes and plans, but that offer us the comfort of continuity, and challenge our resilience and inventiveness in bending old arrangements to present purposes with no outward change. . . . We have, of course, many institutions and arrangements that, as they function, no longer conform to the original scheme, and we have bent most of them quite effectively to the purposes of our present society, which in all respects differs enormously from the society of nearly two hundred years ago. The Supreme Court is one such institution, and the Presidency itself is another. The fact that we have used them without modifying their structures has lent stability to our society and has built strength and confidence in our people.[9]

Defenders stress that, despite some imperfections, the system works. We have not had a popular-vote loser elected by the college in well over a hundred years. The chance of this happening, they say, is not as dangerous as the likely consequences of a move to a direct vote. They quote John F. Kennedy who defended the electoral college by arguing that the question does not merely involve certain technical details of the election process but a whole solar system of subtle, interrelated institutions, principles, and customs. Defenders also quote Lord Falkland's epigram, "when it is not necessary to change, it is necessary not to change," and Livy's pronouncement, "the evil best known is the most tolerable."

Supporters of the electoral college argue that eliminating this fixture would:

- weaken the party system and encourage splinter parties, triggering numerous contingency elections
- undermine the federal system
- lead to interminable recounts and challenges and encourage electoral fraud

- necessitate national control of every aspect of the electoral process
- give undue weight to numbers, thereby reducing the influence of minorities and of the small states
- encourage candidates for president who represent narrow geographical, ideological, and ethnic bases of support
- encourage simplistic media-oriented campaigns and bring about drastic changes in the strategy and tactics used in campaigns for the presidency

Others point out that the elections in 1824 and 1876, in which the popular-vote losers were elected president, had little to do with the electoral college. The present system did not exist in 1824; there was essentially one party and no party convention system that controlled nominations, no popular vote in six states, and no unit electoral vote in six others. Moreover, it was the House of Representatives, not the electoral college, that put in Adams. In 1876, Tilden had a majority in the electoral college, and a rigged electoral commission put in Hayes. Hence, there was only one occasion in over two hundred years, 1888, when the electoral college system denied the popular-vote winner the presidency. Is that reason enough to justify taking a gamble on the direct-vote method?

An additional factor has motivated groups such as the Americans for Democratic Action and the National Association for the Advancement of Colored People (NAACP) to oppose the direct vote and defend the electoral college. One of the few ways American minorities can have an impact on the electoral process is by being the deciding factor in determining which candidate wins a given state and receives its electoral votes. In this way, urban and rural interests, blacks, Latinos, and other minorities can compete for some attention and some share of public policy. If we had direct election of the president, defenders of the electoral college claim, the necessity to take into account the needs and desires of minorities would no longer be as pressing. Candidates could campaign for the American middle and ignore various underrepresented groups. America's minorities could easily suffer. With the direct vote, the weight given to small blocks of voters would be far less than it is today.

Debate on the Two-Party System

Proponents of the electoral college system say it minimizes the impact of minor parties and, because of the unit-rule provision (used by all states except Maine and Nebraska), encourages a politics of moderation. Under the present system losers at party nominating conventions generally abide by their party's choice. With a direct vote, these same losers could be tempted to go after the presidency anyway, hoping to force a runoff election. John Sears, campaign manager for Ronald Reagan's failed presidential bid in 1976, says that if the direct-vote method had been in operation, he would have counseled Reagan to bypass the Republican convention altogether.

Critics of the direct vote suggest that the major parties are, on the national level, only loosely assembled aggregates of state party organizations. Whatever internal discipline they possess comes primarily from their ability to make their nominations stick. They do this primarily because winner-take-all discourages disgruntled losers from launching a campaign on their own. If winner-take-all is removed, say the opponents of direct election, the major parties will lose one of their most potent weapons for enforcing their nominating decisions.

Historian Arthur Schlesinger, Jr., fears that tiny parties or single-cause candidates would be able to magnify their strength through the direct-vote scheme.

> Anti-abortion parties, Black Power parties, anti-busing parties, anti-gun control parties, pro-homosexual-rights parties—for that matter, Communist or Fascist parties—have a dim future in the Electoral College. In direct elections they could drain away enough votes, cumulative from state to state, to prevent the formation of a national majority—and to give themselves strong bargaining positions in a case of a run-off.[10]

Under the present system, the votes for these marginal parties or single-issue candidates have little or no impact, although they sometimes can help one of the major parties and hurt the other. For example, in 1976, independent candidate Eugene McCarthy may have cost Jimmy Carter as many as four states. But under the direct-vote system, each vote cast for a minority party would count. Carried over from state to state, this vote might add up to 19 percent, as the 1992 Perot vote did, or more. This would, it is argued, increase the incentives for these kinds of parties to send a message, register their strength, flex their muscles—and, it is claimed, cause the proliferation of splinter or third parties.

Proponents of the direct vote just as strongly say their plan will not undermine the two-party system. They point out we have a direct vote in the states and that the two-party system is safely intact in the states.

They also assert the two-party system is shaped and sustained not by the electoral college and the winner-take-all provision but by the election of almost all public officials in the United States by single-member districts. Citing the writings of Maurice Duverger, they note that almost every government in the world that elects its officials from single-member districts and by plurality vote has only two major parties, whereas countries that use multimember districts and proportional representation have a multitude of parties.

They point to George Wallace's strategy (even though it failed) in 1968 under the present system. Wallace was encouraged by the electoral-college arrangements to try to carry enough states in a three-way race to enable him to force the two major candidates into a deadlock and bargain with them in the House vote. In effect, the electoral college could sometimes reward regional third parties (like Wallace's American Independent Party) and punish parties with a national constituency. The electoral college system did not discourage independent candidate H. Ross Perot from waging an effective campaign in 1992, in which he captured nearly a fifth of the popular vote (but no electoral votes).

The direct-vote plan stipulates that a candidate must obtain at least 40 percent of the popular vote to win. To prevent that and cause a runoff, a third party or several smaller parties would have to win more than 20 percent of the vote and the two major parties would have to split the rest almost evenly. Says journalist Tom Wicker, "That's no more incentive, and probably less, to a minor party than its chance, under the present system, to prevent an electoral majority and throw a presidential election into the House."[11]

Finally, under the direct-vote system, organizers and supporters of third parties would be able to take votes from the major-party candidate closest to them in policy convictions. Thus, their party could become a spoiler party and thereby ensure the victory of the least-preferred party.

Some contend that with the direct vote we would eliminate the requirement that pluralities be created state by state. This could easily undermine the remaining basis of party competition. The likely result is that more voters would move into the primary of the majority party. Fewer would move into the party of the minority. The minority party would become more extreme until it eventually disappeared.

Debate on Federalism

Defenders of the electoral college say it is part of the subtle structure of federalism, which over the years has thwarted factionalism and helped maintain liberty; to tamper with the electoral college is to tamper with federalism. The electoral college imposes a state-oriented strategy upon presidential candidates. Each candidate must forge a coalition of supporters within each state, especially the big states. To move to a direct vote would lessen the bargaining power of state officials. Countering this argument, others as diverse in their views as Robert Dole and former senator Mike Mansfield say that the federalism issue is phony because the electoral college encourages candidates to ignore noncompetitive states.

If states are abolished as voting units, television campaigning would likely become dominant. Presidential campaign strategy would mainly become a media effort to capture the largest share of the national "vote market." Of course, television is already an essential part of the existing arrangement, but some think it will be relied upon even more in the future, with candidates concentrating on millions of consolidated and easily accessible votes in New York, Los Angeles, Houston, and Chicago. Who needs Wyoming or Idaho? Direct-vote advocates admit major metropolitan areas are advantaged by the electoral college system yet point out that suburbs are advantaged even more.

The federal principle refers not only to the division of responsibilities between nation and states but also to how we currently elect our national officers. The Senate, for example, is entirely a creature of the federal principle, in that each state regardless of its population is granted two seats in the U.S. Senate.

If the states are abolished as voting units for the presidency, centralization would be needed for uniform rules governing challenges and recounts. State laws vary considerably on these matters. For example, may a defeated candidate from a national party convention obtain a ballot listing as a new party or as an independent candidate?

For practical purposes, states would have to yield a certain amount of their constitutionally granted control over the electoral process to some form of federal elections commission. One elections expert raises this point: "The question of candidates' access to the ballot, a technical question in many respects, nevertheless requires a specific definition of political party, a definition on which state laws, court decisions, and political scientists do not agree."[12] Once members of Congress attack details of this nature, they are also likely to regulate further the presidential primary process and the methods of voting, and, hence, at least indirectly, to influence the national conventions. One likely side effect of these new regulations would be that even more states would hold state elections in nonpresidential election years. The trend is already in this direction. If so, the eventual effect of these changes could be a lower turnout of voters in state elections and in presidential elections.

Advocates of the direct vote say one of its virtues is simplicity, but questions of runoff elections and recounts in closely contested elections bother advocates of the present system. Political analysts warn a recount can be a bloody, lengthy, and delayed process. Yet election specialists say a national recount could be accomplished in a reasonably short time, perhaps two weeks or less, and that the recount issue is not paramount.

Defenders of the direct vote contend it would not undermine federalism in any way. "The vitality of federalism," columnist Neal Peirce writes, "rests chiefly on the constitutionally mandated system of congressional representation and the will and capacity of state and local governments to address compelling problems, not on the hocus-pocus of an eighteenth-century vote count system."[13]

Judith Best strongly disagrees with Peirce. She insists the national interest is best defined by a process of consultation, negotiation, and compromise among all of our elected national representatives. And she says the best way to come close to defining America's common good will be to continue to use a federal districting process rather than an all-national headcount.

"Because the president has a powerful voice in defining the national interest," writes Best, "it is just as important for the presidency to be subject to the moderating influence of the federal system as it is the Congress." She adds, "The essential unity of the presidency makes it all the more necessary that the presidency should not be the voice of a private faction."

Debate on Legitimacy

The direct-vote method could easily produce a series of 41-percent presidents, thereby affecting the legitimacy of the winner. Lincoln was the only president with a vote that small, but he wasn't on the ballot in several states. In an era when confidence and trust in the national government have eroded, the direct vote would almost ensure that we would have minority presidents—persons who won with less than 50 percent of the vote—most of the time. We have had sixteen minority presidents, yet the present electoral college system is a two-stage process in which the popular votes are converted into electoral votes. In every election this has the effect of magnifying the vote margin of the winner, so much so that only once in more than a hundred years has a president received less than 55 percent of the electoral college vote (Wilson received 52 percent).

No electoral system is neutral. Trade-offs are very much in evidence in this continuing debate. Electoral college supporters clearly want to discourage third parties and protect a party system that pits one moderate-centrist party against another moderate-centrist party. Moreover, electoral college sympathizers strongly prefer the idea of cross-sectional concurrent majorities. Direct popular vote advocates clearly want all votes to count equally and the candidate with the largest number of popular votes to win. Both schools are concerned with the legitimacy, or public acceptance, of the election process and outcome. As political scientist William Keech notes: "A decision about which system of electing the president to prefer depends on values, on priorities among those values, and on estimates of the likely consequence of change."[14]

There are liabilities or likely adverse effects with both the direct-vote and the electoral college systems. Opponents of the direct vote may have overstated their case. The dire consequences they foresee are probably exaggerated and their view about the role the electoral college plays in maintaining and ensuring the vitality of federalism doubtless gets overstated. Still, they pose enough uncertainty about the possible undesirable side effects of a national direct vote that even the most ardent democratic populist should pause and consider yet other alternatives, other possibilities.

The National Bonus Plan Compromise and Other Alternatives

In the late 1970s, a task force created by the New York-based Twentieth Century Fund (a nonpartisan, not-for-profit foundation) proposed a compromise method of presidential selection that attempted to deal with some of the major problems inherent in both the electoral college and direct election plans.[15] The compromise plan retains the existing 538 state-based electoral votes but adds a national pool of 102 electoral votes that would be awarded on a winner-take-all basis to the candidate who wins at least 40 percent of the popular vote nationwide. There would thus be a combined total of 640 state and national electoral votes, and the candidate with a majority would be the winner. As a consequence, the existing federal bonus in the current electoral college system (of two electoral votes for each state plus the District of

Columbia) would be balanced by this national bonus given to the nationwide popular winner.

This National Bonus Plan, a reform alternative to the existing system, would virtually eliminate the major flaw in the electoral college arrangements. That is, the new system would make it unlikely for the popular-vote winner to lose the election, as happened in 1888 and could have happened in 1960 and 1992.

Because a constitutional amendment is required to establish the National Bonus Plan, a few other changes for simplicity could also be incorporated. Under the National Bonus Plan, there is no need for the office of elector or for the electoral college. The practice of having designated electors would be eliminated and all electoral votes, those now assigned and those proposed under the National Bonus Plan, would be allocated automatically on a winner-take-all basis to the popular-vote winner in each state and in the nation as a whole. Thus, the "faithless elector" problem would be eliminated.

In the unlikely event that no candidate receives a majority of the total electoral vote under the National Bonus Plan, a runoff would be held between the two candidates receiving the most popular votes. This runoff would be held within thirty days of the first national election, and the candidate who won a majority of electoral votes would be elected president. A reasonable alternative would provide for a direct-popular-vote runoff.

These innovations should bring about an improvement in the fairness, and an enhanced public acceptance, of the electoral process without being a drastic or sweeping restructuring of the system. The plan retains some familiar features such as the federal principle, yet it eliminates or minimizes most of the problems that plague the existing presidential election process.

Compared with the existing system, this set of reforms would:

- go a long way toward assuring the election of the candidate with the largest number of popular votes
- reduce the possibility of a deadlock and make the contingency election procedure more representative
- eliminate the so-called faithless elector
- enhance voter equality
- encourage greater voter turnout

As against direct election, it would:

- avoid a proliferation of candidates and help maintain the two-party system

- preserve the federal or cross-sectional character of the presidential election process
- lessen the likelihood of minority presidents
- lessen the likelihood of runoff or second elections
- lessen the likelihood of regional or sectional candidates emerging as major candidates

Thus, this proposed system would remedy most of the problems of the electoral college system and avoid many of the potential problems and risks that might be encouraged with a direct-election process.

Congressman Jonathan Bingham, a New York Democrat, introduced the National Bonus Plan as a constitutional amendment in the 96th Congress and it received several editorial endorsements. However, it won little popular support and was soon forgotten.[16]

The National Bonus Plan may bring to a common position those who advocate direct election of the president and those who support the electoral college. Direct-vote advocates, who believe reform should go all the way to a one-person-one-vote system, may be harder to win over than defenders of the electoral college. Yet one leading direct-vote advocate called the National Bonus Plan an innovative proposal that would break the long-standing logjam on electoral college reform. Though he favors a simple direct-election amendment, he concludes, "between the existing system, with all its perils, and the National Bonus Plan, I find the National Bonus Plan infinitely preferable."[17]

Sooner or later there is going to be another presidential election in which one candidate wins the popular vote but loses the presidency. Or some election will once again have no majority winner of electoral votes and cause the election to be thrown into the House of Representatives for resolution. At that time the furor and heated emotion of the moment may cause a rush to change the system in a radical or overly simplistic way. The National Bonus Plan should at such a time be dusted off and given at least some consideration as a reasonable alternative.

There are, to be sure, obvious drawbacks to this National Bonus Plan. First, it is complicated and is a bit of a Rube Goldberg device. Smaller states would have their vote diluted a bit. Southern states, in general, have a lower turnout and consequently in a nationwide race would lose some voting power to states such as Minnesota, which has high turnout. At least one critic worries that the National Bonus Plan could be deficient in that it might allow a highly sectional base of voting support to win the 102 bonus votes and thereby win the presidential election. The National Bonus Plan is also, in some respects, a direct-vote scheme that is only partially in disguise. Yet, its defenders note, it would help to preserve centrist and two-party politics in the United States, and that might be worth all the trouble.

But the National Bonus Plan is merely one of several alternatives that should be considered. Students of the presidency and the Constitution should examine other possibilities as well, ranging from modest reforms such as eliminating electors, to allocating votes according to some form of proportional representation or approval voting method.[18]

Careful students of presidential elections should begin by trying to develop as rich an understanding as possible of both the existing process, generally known as the electoral college system, and its chief rival the direct, one-person-one-vote plan. The important work of Judith Best—an excellent political scientist—is a sensible place to learn of these plans. The other important and often contrarian essays and documents provided in the last half of this book will also prove instructive.

Their analysis and prescriptions should be, however, only the starting place for bold, imaginative efforts to invent a better way of choosing our presidents. What is needed is the same level of imagination, focus, and long-term appreciation for posterity that the best of our constitutional framers displayed in Philadelphia in the late eighteenth century. In some ways, the constitutional convention of 1787 is still in session. The debates continue. The delegates today are the legal scholars, political writers, judges, legislators, and informed citizens who care enough to reinvent, modify, or reconfirm our political institutions and processes.

THOMAS E. CRONIN is president of Whitman College in Walla Walla, Washington. A political scientist, he is author or coauthor of several books on American politics, including *The State of the Presidency, Direct Democracy*, and *Government by the People*.

Notes

1. Shlomo Slonim, "Designing the Electoral College," in *Inventing the American Presidency*, ed. Thomas E. Cronin (Lawrence: University Press of Kansas, 1989), 33.

2. George F. Will, "The Electoral College's Campus Radical," *Washington Post National Weekly Edition,* 11–17 June 1990, 29. See also Edwin M. Yoder, Jr., "The Electoral College: An Antique That Works" *Washington Star,* 23 March 1978.

3. Yale law school professor Akhil Reed Amar, quoted in *New York Times,* 24 December 1995, E7.

4. Shlomo Slonim, "Designing the Electoral College," 56.

5. Lawrence D. Longley, "Yes, The Electoral College Should Be Abolished," *Controversial Issues in Presidential Selection,* 2nd ed., ed. Gary L. Rose (Albany: SUNY Press, 1994), 206.

6. Nelson Polsby and Aaron Wildavsky, *Presidential Elections,* 9th ed. (Chatham, N.J.: Chatham House, 1995), 292.

7. Stephen J. Wayne, "Let the People Vote Directly for President," in *The Quest for the White House,* ed. Stephen J. Wayne and Clyde Wilcox (New York: St. Martin's Press, 1992), 313–314.

8. *Electing the President: A Report of the Commission on the Electoral College Reform,* Washington, D.C.: American Bar Association, January 1967, 3.

9. Alexander Bickel, "Is Electoral Reform the Answer?" *Commentary Reports* (1968), 3. See also his *New Age of Political Reform* (New York: Harper & Row, 1968).

10. Arthur Schlesinger, Jr., "The Electoral College Conundrum," *Wall Street Journal,* 4 April 1977.

11. Tom Wicker, *New York Times,* 27 March 1977, E17.

12. Richard G. Smolka, "Possible Consequences of Direct Election of the President," *State Government,* summer 1977, 140.

13. Neal R. Peirce, a partial dissent, in *Winner Take All,* Report of the Twentieth Century Fund Task Force on Reform of the Presidential Election Process (New York: Holmes and Meier, 1978), chap. 6.

14. Keech, *Winner Take All,* 67.

15. *Winner Take All.*

16. Jonathan B. Bingham, *Congressional Record,* 26 February 1979, H882–H883. The amendment carried the title, J.H.Res.223.

17. Peirce, *Winner Take All,* 15.

18. See, for example, Douglas Amy, *Real Choices/New Voices: The Case for Proportional Representation Elections in the United States* (New York: Columbia University Press, 1993) and Stephen J. Brams, *The Presidential Election Game* (New Haven: Yale University Press, 1978).

Part One

Why the Electoral College Keeps Winning: The Federal Principle in Presidential Elections

Introduction

As I waited for the elevator, the student approached and asked, "Why does the Electoral College keep on winning?" The elevator had arrived, and I was expected elsewhere. Quickly I answered, "Because the federal principle is just as important in presidential elections as it is in the rest of the Constitution." My regret about the brevity of my answer prompted this effort at a more complete reply.

More constitutional amendments have been proposed to change the Electoral College system of selecting the president than for any other part of the Constitution. Most people, including some political scientists, don't understand how it works or why anyone would say a good word about it. In every presidential election year, one can find numerous editorials calling for its abolition. About every two decades or so there is a fairly strong third-party candidate who, according to the prophets of doom, will deadlock the College and bring disaster to the nation. In between, there are academics with their calculators creating scenarios to prove that even when the last election produced a landslide, it could have produced the "wrong" winner. Congressional committees investigate the issue; prestigious think tanks issue reports and monographs; polls report that a majority of people oppose the College; columnists write "think" pieces; the American Bar Association condemns it; the League of Women Voters launches a national campaign against it. Nonetheless, the Electoral College keeps on winning. As the saying goes, the only difference between a cat and the College appears to be that a cat has only nine lives. But why does the College have so many lives?

As Will Rogers pointed out, "It ain't the things we don't know that hurt us; its the things we know that ain't so." This is particularly true of the electoral vote system. What most of us know "that ain't so" is

3

that the system is undemocratic and therefore indefensible. In fact, the College is both democratic and federal, and therefore it is a model of the American constitutional democracy. The federal principle is one of the fundamental principles of our Constitution. Once we master those principles it is very easy to defend the electoral vote system.

Mastering those principles, however, means unlearning a number of things. One of these things is that simple, direct democracy is the best form of government. Another is that any limit placed on majority rule, or any complex structure designed to give that rule shape and direction, is dangerously illegitimate and must be abolished. To many, complexity is perverse and the term "indirect" smacks of deviousness. And so a political satirist like P.J. O'Rourke seems to hit the mark in his comment about presidential elections.

> The idea seems to be to make the election of the president so complicated and annoying that no one with an important job or a serious avocation— that is, no one presently making any substantial contribution to society— would be tempted to run for the office. So far, it's worked.[1]

But simple is not better than complex when it comes to forms of government. The art of government is like the art of sailing: both have to harness and employ a powerful, changeable, and sometimes turbulent natural force—the wind or the wind of opinion. The wind doesn't always blow toward safe harbor, and so if you would get your ship into port you must tack. To the impatient passenger, the zigzag path, indirect and complex, appears perverse and even dangerous when, in fact, it is actually the safest, surest route.

Most people aren't even aware that the Electoral College exists, much less understand it. When I asked a class what it is, there was silence until one student bravely informed me that it is a small liberal arts college in Pennsylvania. There is nothing particularly shameful in this; things can be useful to us even when we don't fully understand them. When I turn on a light switch, I still tend to think of the result as magic. But if people started claiming that electricity was the work of the devil, I'd make it my business to find out precisely how it worked before I had the power lines to my house disconnected.

The electoral vote system is the most maligned and misunderstood of all of our governing institutions. The American Bar Association has called it "archaic, undemocratic, complex, ambiguous, indirect and dangerous." (The fact that lawyers disapprove of it may be a point in its favor.) The electoral vote system is cast in the role of the political devil, and the people begin to ask why don't we do something about it. Isn't it obviously incompatible with democratic institutions?

This was the kind of question a young Russian interpreter asked me early in the summer of 1991, as we sat on the deck of a boat sailing the Russian waterways from Moscow to what was then Leningrad. He was puzzled about the American system of government. It seemed to him inconsistent, incoherent, and in some ways undemocratic. He cited some of the limits our Constitution places on the majority: the state equality principle in the Senate, our method of amending the Constitution and, especially, presidential elections. It didn't seem like majority rule to him. He asked, "Does American government work," and continued, "I don't understand how." I laughed and responded that some Americans shared his view. "It's messy," I said, "but by and large it does work."

For the next three hours we sat on the deck talking about American government, and what I told him was this. The American government is fundamentally designed to be government by consensus, government that seeks, even though it does not fully achieve, unanimous consent. It was designed to produce liberty and to prevent tyranny, especially majority tyranny. It was designed to create reasonable majorities who can govern because they have the consent of the minority. The question is: why and when would a minority consent to majority rule? The answer is: only if a minority can see that on some occasions and on some important issues it can be part of the majority. It would be irrational to consent to a game in which you can never win, never win anything at all.

Majorities can be tyrannical; the will of the majority is not identical with the common good. Majority rule may be better than minority rule because many heads may be wiser than one or a few—*may be wiser*, not necessarily always will be. Therefore, the bottom line on simple majority rule is that when it is oppressive, fewer people will be oppressed. Faint praise! Clearly a complex governing system that forces majorities to seek the consent of the minority, that doesn't place all power directly and immediately in the hands of the majority, that gives minorities the chance to be part of a majority coalition, is safer and will come closer to the common good.

To allow minorities to be part of a majority, it is necessary to divide both society and government in multiple and complex ways. The federal principle divides society into distinct units, into small societies called states. Majorities must be formed in each of the fifty states and each of the 435 congressional districts in order to fill our national elective offices. This gives minorities of all kinds (racial, religious, ethnic, regional and local, occupational, etc.) many opportunities to be part of a majority, for they may be and often are the swing voters in a districted constituency. As such they must be consulted; their interests must be considered. The federal principle divides government because each elected representative, including the president, is the spokesman for a separately created, federally based majority.

Since there is no all-national majority formed and united by a general election in which the votes of the people are added together wherever they live, majorities must be constructed in Congress in negotiation with the president, day after day, issue by issue. This gives minorities even more opportunities to be a part of a majority coalition. National consensus must be built through consultation, negotiation, and compromise among the delegates sent from the small societies we call states and from segments of these societies. Because of the federal principle, the United States is truly a national society built out of state societies.

To allow minorities to be part of a majority, it is also necessary to have vetoes of various kinds, from the formal presidential veto to the Senate filibuster, because vetoes are not just a way of forbidding a proposal, they also are a way of requiring extraordinary majorities. A veto is a signal that something more must be done to build general agreement and thereby to produce voluntary compliance with the law. It can be a signal that there is something wrong with the proposal, something that must be changed because it places too great a burden on a minority of the people. As the House has an absolute veto over bills passed by the Senate, the Senate has an absolute veto over the bills passed by the House; nothing either chamber passes can become law if the other chamber refuses to pass the bill. In the Senate, the states, large and small, have an equal vote and therefore an opportunity to protect the interests of the citizens of the states as states. And the federally elected president has a qualified veto—one that can be overridden by an extraordinary majority in Congress. Our Constitution seeks to approach national consensus by giving state-affiliated minorities a voice and some form of qualified veto. It thereby creates federal public minorities rather than purely arithmetical private ones, and it uses these federal public minorities as the building blocks of a broadly inclusive national majority.

My thesis is simple. The electoral vote system is the very model of our federal system. If the federal principle is legitimate (and I think it is) then it is just as legitimate in the selection of the president as in the selection of the Congress. If it is not, then it should be abandoned throughout the Constitution.

The friends of democratic government, misunderstanding the nature of the case, reject the federal principle in presidential elections and promote the power of the all-national, numerical majority in the mistaken belief that this will make the government more popular— more responsive to the will of the people. What it actually does is make the government less popular. The will of the people is not the same as the will of the numerical majority, for the majority are only a part of the people. The goal of American government is much higher than majority rule; it is majority rule with the consent of the minority. These are two very different things, and the federal principle, even and especially in presidential elections, is essential to achieving minority consent.

Notes

1. P.J. O'Rourke, *Parliament of Whores* (New York: Random House, 1992), 13–14.

Chapter 1

Do We Have a Winner?

As the Perot candidacy built up strength in the spring of 1992, the media forecasters began to sound the alarm. Perot would be more than a spoiler for one of the two major party candidates; he would be the ultimate spoiler, the process spoiler, the candidate who deadlocked the Electoral College, triggering the nightmare of a contingency election in the House of Representatives. In April, Doug Bailey warned in the *Wall Street Journal* that 1992 could be the year that Congress picked a president. In May, the *New York Times Magazine* published Norman Ornstein's fascinating fantasy about a Bill Bradley presidency emerging from the House contingency election. At the end of May, *USA Today*, under a banner opinion-page headline reading "Electoral Nightmare Looms," printed Elizabeth McCaughey's proposals to avert a crisis.

By early summer quite a number of people were in a state of panic. Some state legislators were considering immediate changes in state laws governing the allocation of electoral votes. At least three constitutional amendments on presidential selection were proposed in the U.S. Senate, and two Senators, each proposing a different amendment, said they hoped their amendment could take effect before the November 1992 election. To even suggest changing the rules of the game when the game is already underway is truly panic. To do that would destroy the people's confidence in the legitimacy of the election. Whoever won would have to live with charges of a stolen election. Senator Paul Simon, Chairman of the Subcommittee on the Constitution of the Senate Judiciary Committee, held hearings on the various proposals to change the method of selecting the president, and I was among those invited to testify.

Panic subsided when, in July, Perot abruptly withdrew from the race, blaming the Electoral College. He said his candidacy would deadlock the electoral votes and noted, "putting this thing in the House of Representatives is negative and disruptive and we shouldn't do it."[1] Whatever his reason for withdrawing in July, fear of deadlock wasn't it because Perot re-entered the race at the eleventh hour. I had predicted to the Senate Subcommittee and to various reporters that if Perot ran there would be a landslide electoral vote victory for one of the two major party candidates, and on election night I was vindicated. In the wake of Clinton's victory, I looked in vain for newspaper stories like the following:

The Electoral College Wins Again!

Stunning the pundits and pollsters, the veteran Electoral College rallied to a landslide victory. Final electoral vote score: Clinton 69 percent; Bush 31 percent; pundits, pollsters, and Perot zero. In what many predicted could be its greatest challenge in this century, the electoral vote system was pitted against three challengers, and since one was a billionaire, the odds-makers speculated the College would lose. On election day, however, the much-maligned College, in an easy victory, added to its winning streak. It produced a single election, gave the victory to the winner of a broadly based popular plurality, supported our moderate two-party system, and, most important, preserved and fortified the federal principle.

Why did the Electoral College win again? Why was there no triggering of the contingency election system? Why was there no deadlock? The simple answer is the federal principle in presidential elections. The more complex answer is the magnifier effect of the state unit rule, also known as the winner-take-all rule. To win the presidency a candidate must win states, and every state has as many electoral votes as it has representatives in Congress. With two exceptions, Maine and Nebraska, our individual presidential votes are counted in state-sized boxes, and the candidate who wins a statewide plurality wins all of the state's electoral votes. If a candidate wins 53 percent of the popular vote in New York, or even a mere plurality, he wins New York. He wins 100 percent of New York's electoral votes. In 1992 that was 33 electoral votes.

The unit rule is the cause of the magnifier effect. This is why the victor in the presidential election will have a higher percentage of the electoral vote than he does in the popular vote. Here are two recent examples to illustrate the magnifier effect. In 1976 Carter won 50.1

percent of the total popular vote and 55 percent of the total electoral vote. In 1984 Reagan won 58.8 percent of the total popular vote and 98 percent of the total electoral vote.

The magnifier effect is an undeniable fact; its consequences, however, are often misunderstood. Some claim it misrepresents the popular will and overstates the mandate. They think it is a kind of fisherman's story in which the size of the fish caught grows with the telling. The fact is that it serves to create a proper mandate but does not exaggerate it. It helps to catch the fish, not to lie about how big it is. Two factors are necessary to create a mandate: a sufficient percentage of the *popular votes* and a broadly based federal distribution of those popular votes. The magnifier effect serves to ensure the latter for it creates candidate incentives necessary to build a broadly based victory.

Like fish, mandates come in various sizes. Some mandates are whoppers, others are barely keepers. The magnifier effect does not convert small fry into trophy fish; it does not hide the difference between a merely sufficient mandate and a powerful one, between Clinton's 43 percent and Franklin Roosevelt's 60.7 percent of the popular vote. For a powerful mandate, a true landslide, most political scientists agree that, at minimum, a candidate must win 55 percent of the popular vote and, of course, that 55 percent must be federally distributed. A candidate who wins 60 percent of the popular vote and all of it cast east of the Mississippi or north of the Mason-Dixon line not only doesn't have a powerful mandate, but, it can be argued, doesn't have a mandate at all.

Powerful mandates are uncommon. There have been only fourteen since 1832, when the current system of popular elections in which the winner-takes-all electoral-votes rule evolved. Even when a candidate wins 55 percent of the popular vote or more, the mandate is a temporary thing that must be continually reinforced. An election is a snapshot of the will of the electorate. To the extent it is accurate, its accuracy is for that day. The will of the electorate can be very different a few months or even weeks later. In 1932, Franklin D. Roosevelt was given a mandate on promises to do one thing. He did the opposite and was re-elected in 1936 with a greater mandate. In terms of mandates we should think about the story of the little girl who asked her father, "Do all fairy tales begin with: once upon a time?" "Well no," her father answered. "Some of them begin with: when I'm elected."

The magnifier effect not only helps to catch the fish—to create a properly distributed sufficient base of popular support—it also helps to bring it safely to shore before it begins to rot. It does this by making the general election the only election, by preventing deadlocks and thus resort to contingency elections.

The fear of deadlock arises when there are three or more candidates with strong popular followings. Normally there are five or six so-called "third-party" candidates in a presidential election. In 1960 there were thirteen. The only relevant third-party candidacies are the ones that can win states, that can win electoral votes. When I gave my testimony in July of 1992, there had been five elections in our history when there were three or more strong contenders who won some electoral votes. In every case the electoral vote system magnifier effect not only gave the victory to the winner of the popular plurality, it created an electoral vote landslide for that candidate. As long as the state unit rule remains in effect, third-party candidacies won't create deadlocks; they create electoral vote landslides.

In 1992, Perot won 19 percent of the popular vote, second highest in this century for a third-party candidate, but *he did not win a single electoral vote because he did not win a single state*. He could not deadlock the election unless he could win some states. The media paid little attention to the necessity of winning states, and thus they panicked. Often they reported Perot's support on a national not a state-by-state basis, thus ignoring the election laws. It would be as though the sports reporters told us that the Cubs would get into the World Series because, in terms of hits rather than league games won, they were one of the top two teams in all of baseball. You've got to understand the rules before you can accurately report on the game.

TABLE 1.1

Years When Third Party Won Electoral Votes: Popular and Electoral (in italics) Vote Percentages

1856	Buchanan	Fremont	Fillmore	
	45.4 *58.7*	33	21.6	
1860	Lincoln	Douglas	Breckinridge	Bell
	39.79 *59.4*	29.4	18.1	12.6
1912	Wilson	Roosevelt	Taft	
	41.85 *81.9*	27.4	23.2	
1924	Coolidge	Davis	La Follette	
	54.1 *71.7*	28.8	16.6	
1968	Nixon	Humphrey	Wallace	
	43.4 *55.9*	42.7	13.5	

But what about a deadlock strategy? Perot may not have been seeking to deadlock the Electoral College, but in 1968 George Wallace was. He collected affidavits from his electors that pledged them to vote for him or the man of his choice in the College. The 1968 election illustrates the impracticality of a deadlock strategy. To bring off such a strategy a candidate must walk a very narrow path.

> First he must have a strong base in some states where he can win electoral votes. Then he must wage a national campaign for popular votes that produces a fairly even electoral vote division between the two major party candidates in order to prevent the stronger candidate from getting an electoral majority. If the major parties are evenly matched in potential electoral votes, he must draw equally on the strength of both. If they are not, he must draw more from the stronger. But during the course of the campaign the relative positions of the two major party candidates continuously fluctuate. The third-party candidate with a deadlock strategy is in the situation of a parachutist attempting to land on a dime with the winds strong and variable.[2]

And so in 1968, when George Wallace won 13.5 percent of the popular vote, he won only 8 percent of the electoral vote, and Nixon's popular vote plurality of 43.4 percent was magnified into 55.9 percent of the electoral vote. There was no deadlock. And there will be no deadlock as long as the magnifier effect is in place.

This is comforting because it is hard to find anyone who approves of the current contingency procedure. If no presidential candidate wins a majority of the electoral votes, the House of Representatives must choose from among the top three winners of electoral votes. In this election, however, each state will have only one vote and the successful candidate must win a majority of the states. The quorum necessary for this House election is at least one member from two-thirds of the states.

There are real problems with this plan. First, it is possible that the president and vice president would be members of different parties. If no candidate for the vice presidency wins a majority of the electoral votes, a different body, the Senate, must choose the vice president and then only from among the top two winners of vice presidential electoral votes. Second, it is possible that the presidential candidate who won a popular vote plurality would lose in the House, if he belonged to the House minority party. Third, there is the possibility of secret and corrupt deals between candidates and members of the House, or even the suspicion of such deals. Fourth, there is the possibility of delay and uncertainty even beyond inauguration day either because no candidate can win a majority of states, or if one can, because his opponents control enough states to prevent a quorum, for without a quorum the vote cannot be taken.

Some but not all of these problems can be solved by other kinds of contingency elections, such as a popular vote runoff, but all of them create additional problems. For example, a popular vote runoff would solve the first two problems but not the last two. Whenever the general election fails, there is always the possibility of secret and corrupt deals because the candidates in the runoff will be seeking the support of those knocked out, and those knocked out will be seeking something in exchange for their endorsements. And since there must be a trigger for a runoff—some minimal percentage of the total popular vote and/or its distribution—there can be disputes about whether that minimal percentage has been met. This means delay and prolonged uncertainty. And because it creates a second chance psychology in both voters and candidates, a popular runoff provision will make runoffs the rule and not a rare exception.

What we have is a situation where we have no real problem, and we know why we don't—the magnifier effect of the federal winner-take-all rule. We are offered solutions to this "problem" that don't actually solve it but instead make it more likely that the problem will become a permanent condition. Suppose your father is partially bald. It is possible that you too will become partially bald, though there is no sign of it. So you start using hair restorers, but it turns out you are allergic to them, and all your hair falls out. We have never had a contingency election since the magnifier effect has been in place. This is one good reason to place the cause of the magnifier effect—the state unit rule, also known as the winner-take-all system—in the Constitution.

The magnifier effect is a hard fact, but what is its political value? Its value is that it produces a definite, accepted winner who can govern. It gives us a single election and a decision that is swift, sure, clean, and clear. We don't want contingency elections. We don't want delay, uncertainty, and an incentive for secret deals as candidates maneuver for support after the general election fails. We don't want to have the outcome in doubt for weeks or even months as a contingency election process drags on or as challenges to the general election count and then to a runoff election count are raised in every voting precinct. This could degenerate into a situation in which two candidates claim victory, name their cabinet officers, and make policy statements while the world watches in dismay. This would be bad enough in terms of our domestic politics, but think of the impact of such uncertainty on our foreign policy! Think merely of what Saddam Hussein and others of his ilk would do to take advantage of such an interregnum!

The electoral vote system, *in practice*, is a direct, federal, popular plurality system that magnifies the plurality winner's margin of victory over the runner-up, effectively providing us with a single election—no need for a contingency election. In the 160 years since the current system has been in place, we have never had a deadlock, we have never had a contingency election nor come close to one, even in the closest popular elections. This is one reason why the Electoral College keeps on winning.

Notes

1. *USA Today*, 17 July, 1992.
2. Judith A. Best, *The Case Against Direct Election of the President: A Defense of the Electoral College* (Ithaca: Cornell University Press, 1975), 98–99.

Chapter 2

The Right Winner:
Not By Numbers Alone!

Often as people walk out of a sporting event you will hear them say, "Well, the right team won!" Many will say this even if their own team lost. These are people who understand that the game is a test of strength, speed, skill—of the comparative worth of the two teams. Putting personal preference aside, they were able to see that one team was stronger on defense, quicker and more accurate on offense, and so concluded that the final score reflected the quality of play. Like a game, an election is a process, and the proof of any process is its product. Does the federal electoral vote system produce the right winner?

Its critics say no. They charge that the system is undemocratic because they claim that it is quite likely to produce the "wrong" winner—to give the presidency to a candidate who was the runner-up in the popular vote. They point out that it has done so once in 1888, when Cleveland outpolled Harrison in the popular vote by eight-tenths of 1 percent but lost in the electoral vote. They also create numerous scenarios suggesting that in many elections a shift of a small number of votes in a few states could have made the runner-up the president. Their principle of democratic legitimacy is numbers alone—their only standard for determining the right winner is the law of the greater part. Because there is a risk of a runner-up president, they say the current system is indefensible.

On the contrary, the system is quite easy to defend, and their principle of legitimacy is challengeable as inadequate on political grounds. Their principle boils down to: the majority must win, and the minority must lose no matter what they lose. Time was, when an arithmetical majority in this country supported slavery or at least racial discrimination. The pages of history contain many examples of oppressive rulers who enjoyed the support of an arithmetical majority. The majority can be wrong; the majority can willfully oppress a minority. For this reason, the framers took every precaution they could think of to prevent majority tyranny. Nonetheless, there are risks in our presidential election system. But since risks are taken in order to gain some otherwise unattainable advantage, we must consider the ratio of risk to benefit. How often does the electoral vote system produce a runner-up president? Under what circumstances? What is the benefit sought? Is the benefit worth the risk?

Defending the "Indefensible"

To begin with the often unrecognized obvious, politics and mathematics are two very different disciplines. Mathematics seeks accuracy, politics seeks harmony. In mathematics an incorrect count loses all value once it is shown to be wrong. In politics even though some people are out-voted they still have value and must be respected in defeat. Efforts must be made to be considerate and even generous to those who lost the vote, to make them feel they are part of the community, for if they feel alienated they may riot in the streets. Further, mathematical questions, like those in all the sciences, deal with truth and falsehood. But politics is an art, not a science. Political questions do not deal primarily with truth and falsehood, but with good and bad. We do not ask whether a political decision on war or taxation or welfare or agricultural subsidies is true. We ask, is the policy good for the country? And, will it actually achieve its purpose?

   Those who confuse politics and mathematics, the head counters, operate on an unstated assumption that the will of the people is out there like some unsurveyed land, and all we need do is send out the surveyors with accurately calibrated instruments to record what is there. They also assume that our democratic republic is a ship without a specific destination. Whatever most of the people want, most of the people must get, and the minority be damned. Mathematical accuracy being their sole criterion for legitimacy, they make a great fuss about politically imposed devices, intermediary institutions like the electoral vote system with its federal principle and its winner-take-all rule. From their perspective, such majority building and structuring devices complicate their self-assigned task, distort the accuracy of their count, and possibly produce the "wrong" result.

If their assumptions were correct they would have a point. But their assumptions are false. Ours is a ship of state bound for a port called Liberty. On such a ship majority rule doesn't suffice without the consent of the minority. Their assumption about the will of the people is particularly false in this vast and varied country, in a continental republic populated by a people who do not share a common religion, race, or ethnic heritage, in a commercial republic populated by people with diverse and competing economic interests. In such a country the will of the people and the will of the majority can be two very different things. Therefore, the will of the people—that one thing which all can share, which is the goal of liberty for all—must be constructed and periodically reconstructed. This requires a political, not a mathematical, process.

Minority Presidents

The political process must be recognized as democratically legitimate. But what is a legitimate democratic process? The word "legitimate" means lawful, in accordance with established rules and standards. The word "democratic" refers to a governing system in which power resides in all the people and provides for the benefit of all. So to be legitimate, the rules of a democratic process must be decided in advance, be the same for all, applied to all. And in a democratic process the majority rules.

Strictly speaking, this means that the office should not go to the candidate who wins a mere plurality. A plurality victory requirement produces the "wrong" winner—a minority president. This being the case, quite a few of our presidents cannot be called the right winner, for sixteen of them have been minority presidents—they did not win a majority of the popular vote. The list includes some of our greatest presidents: Wilson, Truman, and, above all, Lincoln, who polled the lowest popular vote percentage of any winner in our history, a mere 39.79 percent. It also includes Kennedy, Nixon, and Bill Clinton.

Sixteen out of forty-two, that's a great risk of a minority president! Why are we so lax about the majority rule principle? If the right winner is the one who polls a popular-vote majority then, whenever no candidate achieved this, we could have a popular vote runoff. But runoffs are expensive, take a lot of time, and ironically may increase our disagreements rather than our unity. Enough is enough. As it is, the election process extends into well over a year. There comes a time when even the players want the game to be over and so accept some otherwise questionable way to determine victory, like a sudden-death rule in football or a shoot-out in hockey. Rigidity on the democratic majority principle strikes most of us as ideological. We are a practical people and seem to be satisfied if we can fill the office in a timely fashion with the winner of a reasonably sufficient plurality. There can be good, principled reasons for modifying the principle of the arithmetical majority. Even the head counters appear to recognize that a victory requirement that defeats a basic purpose of having elections—filling the office in an undisputed and timely fashion—is absurd. It would seem the right winner is not simply the candidate with a majority, but the one with the most votes.

It is so important to fill the office in a timely fashion that we are willing to compromise that principle much further. We accept as president a person who has not won a single popular vote in a national election. Gerald R. Ford, our thirty-eighth president, succeeded to the office on the resignation of Richard Nixon. Ford had been nominated by Nixon to fill a vice presidential vacancy and was confirmed by a majority vote of both houses of Congress under the provisions of the Twenty-fifth Amendment.

The Runner-up President

A minority president is one thing but a runner-up president is quite another. And what causes this aberration? The answer is the electoral vote system with its winner-take-all principle, for it gives all of a state's electoral votes to the winner of a state-wide plurality. This means that a candidate's popular vote percentage will be different from his electoral vote percentage. In every case but one it has given extra electoral votes to the candidate who won the most popular votes. But this means that the runner-up in the popular vote can win the office. The loser wins! When we put it that way it's more than irregular—it's wrong.

But is it always clearly and completely wrong? If one candidate polled a definitive majority of the popular votes and the runner-up got the office, the outcome would be clearly wrong. An electoral system that does this frequently is simply indefensible. (The current electoral vote system has never done this. It has never turned the winner of a popular vote majority into a loser.) Other cases are not so clear, for all runner-up situations are not the same. There is more than one kind of runner-up. There is a difference between being the second-place finisher in a blow-out and in a squeaker. There is a difference between being the runner-up to a plurality winner and to a majority winner.

The plurality winner's right to the office is somewhat questionable to begin with, for a majority of the people did not support him. It becomes even more questionable if the plurality falls below 40 percent of the popular vote. Does a plurality of 20 or 30 percent of the popular vote create a right to the office? When 70 percent of the voters have not supported a candidate, it's ridiculous to say he is the democratically right winner simply because he received the most votes. Further, if the plurality is small—if the margin between the candidates is fractional—the right of the plurality winner begins to disappear.

Politics is more like horseshoes than speed skating—close matters. In 1960, Kennedy won 49.71 percent of the popular vote, and Nixon won 49.55 percent. With a margin of less than two-tenths of 1 percent of the votes separating the two candidates, quite a few people would have quarreled with the assertion that Kennedy was clearly the right winner (especially since there were believable charges of fraud in both Texas and Illinois, both of which Kennedy narrowly carried for a combined total of fifty-one electoral votes). Commentators pointed to the fact that Kennedy won eighty-four more electoral votes than Nixon as a justifiable "tie" breaker. And in presidential elections we need one. In the 1994 Winter Olympics, when Nancy Kerrigan finished second in figure skating on the basis of a one-tenth point difference, it seemed to many that the contest was really a draw and that two gold medals should have been awarded. Perhaps that could be possible in the Olympics, but we can't have two presidents.

In this light let us examine the risk of a runner-up presidency under the electoral vote system. We have had only one runner-up president, Benjamin Harrison, and that happened when no candidate won a popular vote majority, and the election was so close as to be a dead heat. The system has never stolen the victory from the undisputed winner of a popular majority.

We cannot say John Quincy Adams was a runner-up president in 1824, because only half of the states were employing the current system, and in one quarter of the states there was no popular vote at all. Since we can't know what the national popular vote would have been in 1824, the "wrong" winner concept is meaningless in that election year. Nor can we say that the election of 1876 produced the "wrong" winner in Hayes, for there was such widespread fraud on both sides and such voter intimidation practiced by Tilden's party that the election can't be called free and fair. It is a travesty of the democratic principle to argue about popular vote percentages when the election is not free and fair, when there are threats and whippings and shootings and murders that prevent people from casting their votes.

There may have been only one runner-up president, but one is too many, and no one can say there will never be another unless we change the system. For those who confuse politics with arithmetic, that statement is conclusive. But political authority isn't just a matter of having the most votes. In politics as well as in physics there is such a thing as a critical mass. The mass of popular support must be sufficient to authorize, to give title to office. The question is: What is the nature of this critical mass in presidential elections? Part of it is numbers of votes, and part of it is the *distribution* of those votes. Numbers are not enough in a heterogeneous continental nation if we are interested in more than filling the office, if we want to make certain that the office holder can govern, if we want a president who represents more than just one region of the country.

Imagine the following scenario. On election night as we watch the returns on television, we see the map of the United States, and the networks color each state red as the people in a state choose Ed Easterbrook or blue as they choose Will Westfail. If the eastern half of the country is all red and the western half is all blue, it could be an ominous result. Every politically savvy person will sit up to look at the state-by-state popular vote percentages. Easterbrook is winning the states in the East by huge margins; none by under 80 percent and in some cases by over 90 percent. He is losing to Westfail in the other half of the country by the same margins. The western states are aptly colored blue, for Easterbrook wins the presidency. This is a formula for civil war.

If we change the scenario a little the results are not so ominous. Let's make Easterbrook's margins in the East 52 to 53 percent, and he is losing by the same margins in the West. Not terrific but tolerable. It still doesn't look great for the prospects of governing, but it's a vast improvement. Let's change the scenario a little more; this time Easterbrook is winning a few states in the West with 51 or 52 percent; let's make it six or seven out of nineteen states. Now, despite the close margins, we have a president who can govern. This is not a powerful mandate, but his support is sufficiently widespread so that he can claim to represent the nation in its diversity. He has a legitimate claim to being president of the whole country.

The right winner is the one who gets the most votes if his votes are properly distributed—if he has sufficient support in all parts of the country. The right winner is the candidate with a *federal* plurality. Bill Clinton may be a minority president with 43 percent of the popular votes, but he won thirty-two states, and he won states in all regions of the country. The federal nature of his victory buttressed an otherwise barely sufficient popular vote percentage.

The next question is: What produces the last scenario instead of the first? The answer is the same thing that makes a runner-up president possible though not likely—the federal election and the state laws that give all of a state's electoral votes to the candidate who wins the most votes within the state. To win the presidency a candidate must win a majority of the electoral vote, and to do this he must win states, lots of them and not just the states in one region of the country. And to win lots of states he wants to make certain that his popular-vote support is properly distributed.

Since a candidate can win Pennsylvania or Georgia with 51 percent of the popular votes in those states, or even with a simple plurality, it is foolish for a candidate to try to win 80 percent there at the expense of votes in other states. He gets 100 percent of a state's electoral vote with a simple majority or a plurality; he gets no extra electoral votes by carrying a state with 80 percent of its popular votes. The extra effort to do this would be more wisely expended in additional states. California may have 54 electoral votes, but if a candidate is projected to win there with 60 to 65 percent of the vote, he doesn't want to spend more of his resources in time, promises, and money trying to increase his percentage there. It would be overkill. He would be better advised to spend his resources elsewhere in states that are considered too close to call, even if those states have only three or four electoral votes.

In the National Football League, to get into the playoffs and thus to win the Super Bowl, a team has to win games just as a presidential candidate has to win states. Why don't we forget about winning games and let teams get into the playoffs on the basis of the total number of points they score during the regular season? If we did this what would happen? Teams would have the incentive to run up the score against their weakest opponents. Teams in the most competitive divisions, teams that play the best football, would have the least chance to get into the playoffs.

If we abandon the electoral vote system, if we say to candidates you don't have to win states, all you have to do is win the most votes, what will they do? One strategy is to run a sectional campaign, to promise everything to the populous Eastern megalopolis; run up the score, run up the votes with them, and to hell with the rest of the country. Now there is a formula for inability to govern. Or a candidate could promise everything to the suburbanites, who are half of all the voters, and forget about the urban and rural voters. Or he could promise everything to white Christians. This is a formula for majority tyranny. And the best candidates—the candidates who can build the broad political coalitions that are essential for a president to govern—would lose to those who could gain the overwhelming support of a narrow, exclusive group of the people.

If we abandon the win-games rule, noncontender teams that could rise to the occasion and defeat a contender in a close contest wouldn't be recognized. When all that matters is total points scored in the season, a loss by a narrow margin to a team that is not a contender wouldn't matter. If we abandon the win-states rule in presidential elections, groups like farmers, who are only 2 percent, or blacks, who are only 12 percent of the national voting population, won't get much attention or have much influence. But when candidates have to win states, such minorities have influence. Candidates have to take them seriously because they could be the swing voters in a closely divided state.

An election system that provides an organized minority with more attention than its raw numbers alone would warrant can be a consensus-building device. As such it is also a legitimizing force precisely because it gives minorities an opportunity they otherwise would not have—the opportunity to help form the majority. And the only reason a minority would consent to majority rule is if on occasion they can be part of the majority. Nor is this kind of device a novelty in our system. There are many constitutional rules that provide minorities with more influence than their numbers alone would warrant, including the extraordinary majority of three-fourths for passing constitutional amendments and the state equality principle in casting the votes on amendments. All of these rules have national harmony as their goal.

Those who confuse politics with arithmetic assume that if we abolished the federal principle, if we directly added my vote in New York with my mother's vote in Michigan, my oldest son's vote in Arizona, and my youngest son's vote in Virginia, nothing else would change or would change for the worse. But when you change the rules, you change the game, and you change the game plans, and you change the skills needed to win. They would change the rules because these rules make it possible, but very unlikely, for a runner-up to become president.

It is very unlikely for the same reason that football coaches don't try to run up the score in a game they have good reason to believe they have already won, for the same reason that they don't leave in their starting quarterback and great fullback when they are ahead late in the fourth quarter by at least three touchdowns. These essential players might get hurt for nothing, and thus running up the score in this game may cost them the victory in other games. It is more important to win other games than to boast of beating this team by five touchdowns. Coaches know the rules for getting into the Super Bowl; they know that trying to run up the score in this game could result in hurting their chances to win in other games. Candidates and political parties know the same kind of thing in presidential elections; they do know the rules of the electoral vote system; they will try to win the most states rather than a few states by overwhelming margins.

Because of the winner-take-all rule, the electoral vote system is essentially a plurality system. It magnifies the plurality winner's margin of victory in the electoral vote. Thus in 1992, Clinton won 43 percent of the popular vote but 69 percent of the electoral vote. In every case but one it has worked to the advantage of the winner of the national popular vote. The exception was the election of 1888, when no candidate polled a majority, and when Harrison won the election though Cleveland beat him in the popular vote by eight-tenths of one percent. Eight-tenths of one percent! An election this close is or verges on a draw. And why did the magnifier effect fail in this one case? Because Cleveland ran a sectional campaign. He won southern states by huge margins and lost some northern states very narrowly because he beat on the sectionally divisive tariff drum. He didn't try to broaden his base and develop greater support in the northern states. No, he chose to campaign on an issue that hurt him in the North where he needed help, on an issue that helped him in the South where he didn't. He tried to run up the score in states he had already won, and it cost him other states he might have won if he had considered how important it was to broaden his base.

If anything, the election of 1888 provides proof that the electoral vote system rewards candidates who create broad, inclusive, national coalitions and punishes candidates who don't. Remember 1888! This ought to be the watchword of all our presidential campaigns. The electoral vote system provides both the carrot and the stick. It punishes candidates who pursue a narrow but deep strategy and rewards those who pursue a broadly cross-national one. The fact that the runner-up has been elected only once indicates that the candidates have figured out the system of rewards and punishments.

But the head counters contend, despite the historical evidence to the contrary, that the current system is very dangerous and could have often produced a runner-up president. (Please note, however, they give no explanation as to why it hasn't.) They create a series of shift-in-votes scenarios to suggest that we have only narrowly avoided such catastrophes in many election years. They create such scenarios by treating voters as numbers that are easily moved from one column to another. They say *if* there had been a shift of less than 1 or 2 percent in the popular vote, there would have been a runner-up president in this election and all these others.

In creating these scenarios, some of them ignore the election laws and define their percentages as if the shift in the vote were to be cast nationally rather than in a single state or a few states. This is like saying the New York Giants would have played in the 1994 Super Bowl if they had scored three or four more touchdowns during the regular season, without specifying the games in which those extra touchdowns had to be scored.

All of them blithely assume an exact number of votes that would shift, and then to compound this nonsense, they assume that the shifts in this precise number of votes would occur only in some specific states and not in any others. They move these numbers of votes around in a political vacuum as if votes were cast randomly and arbitrarily. They do not give a political reason (a campaign promise, a scandal, a foreign policy crisis, an endorsement from a powerful factional leader, a slip of the tongue during a televised debate) for this imagined shift in votes. One can suggest political reasons for a shift in votes in any election: if Bush had not broken his "no new taxes" promise, if Carter's rescue of the American hostages in Iran had been successful, if Ford had not pardoned Nixon and knew that Poland was not then part of the free world.

Failure to provide a political reason reduces the possibility of rational discussion. It is hard to imagine a political reason for vote shifts that would be confined to the one state or only the few states that would produce a runner-up president. Political reasons for vote shifts would not be confined only to those states that would produce a runner-up president, they would extend to the whole country. They would probably change the name of the winner, but they would not produce a runner-up president. If Bush had not broken his "read my lips, no new taxes" promise, he might have won. If Carter's rescue plan for our hostages in Iran had been successful, he might have won. The shift-in-votes argument doesn't work because voters aren't numbers, and you can't just shift a few of them from one column to another without explaining what would have caused this shift by only these voters in this state and not other voters in other states.

As a parlor game to amuse academics this is all good fun. But when real folks who ordinarily have common sense start to pay attention to this its time for a reality check. I hope one example suffices. One recently concocted scenario of the 1988 election makes Dukakis the runner-up president "if fewer than one percent of the nation's voters, concentrated in those eleven states, had shifted their votes from Bush to Dukakis."[1] This is an election that verged on a popular vote landslide for Bush, who won 54 percent of the popular vote to Dukakis's 46 percent.

To make their case they provide three tables of numbers, and just to give you the flavor, they assume a precise 1.6 percent shift of votes in California, a 4.1 percent shift of votes in Michigan, and a 3.2 shift of votes in South Dakota. In each of the eleven states the percentage must be no more and no less than predicted—that is to say, if Glinda, the good witch of the North, waved her magic wand! There are eleven of these precise assumptions built one upon the other. If any one of them were off target the whole fantasy fails.

I sure wouldn't want one of these shift-in-votes guys to be my stock broker. If X number of people sell this stock, and if Y number of people buy this second stock, and if Z number of people neither buy nor sell this third stock—if and only if all these three things happen on the same day—you will make money. I can't give you any reason why all these people will do these different things but just look at my numbers. They add up!

Are there good reasons for a system that possibly could give the victory to the runner-up? Yes there are, if this occurs very rarely and only in an election that verges on a tie. Two good reasons are: the system promotes national harmony and establishes a political rather than a merely arithmetical qualification for the presidency. Are these benefits worth the risk? Yes if we want to create an incentive for candidates to build the broad, moderate, cross-national coalitions necessary for governing. Presidential elections systems are and must be complex because they have several purposes, among which are filling the office in a timely basis and creating a political critical mass of support that authorizes the president to govern, a critical mass that, in this country, is a combination of sufficient popular votes and a national distribution of those popular votes.

One Voter, One Vote

Who is the right winner? Those who confuse politics with arithmetic not only believe the right winner is the candidate who wins the most votes no matter how they are distributed, but also that the right winner is produced by a process in which all citizens not only have one vote, they also have equal political influence. That is a utopian dream. No political system can provide that because human beings are not clones of each other, because we have different talents and live in different circumstances. There are all kinds of things that make for political influence: a silver tongue, a face the camera loves, intelligence, celebrity status, wealth, reputation, a quick wit, a certain family name—like Kennedy, or a particular occupation (a newspaper reporter has more political influence than the carpenter who lives down the street).

To achieve the end of equal political influence on the presidency, the head counters say we must adopt a direct nonfederal election, for only that will give us one man, one equally weighted vote. But their direct, nonfederal election proposal doesn't provide that. It only provides for one voter, one vote, and even then the votes aren't equally weighted—equally powerful and influential—because human beings aren't isolated agents; they form groups.

Group formation is a fundamental fact of human life, and individual voting choices are affected by perceptions of relative group influence. Individual voters form alliances with others and work together to get out the group vote: to get out the black vote, or the Catholic vote, or the labor vote. And candidates aren't influenced by raw numbers of voters, but by their perceptions of relative voting-bloc solidarity, and thence by calculations about which voting blocs can be joined into a statewide winning coalition. Some groups, and thus the individuals within those groups, will have more influence than others because their goals are more compatible with the goals of other groups. Not all groups are equal in political influence, and group influence, like individual influence, is produced by a number of variable factors, such as group size, distribution, prestige, cohesion, and the zeal of the group's members.

Further, those who confuse politics with arithmetic and demand one voter, one equally weighted vote, ignore the fact that many people do not vote, and that to refuse to cast a vote can be a "vote" by other means. A prominent political scientist, Theodore Lowi, once publicly advised people not to vote as a political act of protest. A refusal to formally cast a ballot can be a vote for none of the above. Some people think that voting "just encourages the bastards," others that "there's not a dime's worth of difference" among the candidates. An election boycott is a political act and one that can be very powerful. Not only does it draw attention to the demands of the boycotting group, if the boycott is sufficiently large, it can also weaken the presidency or destroy the legitimacy of the election. Every vote that is not cast may be interpreted as a vote of no confidence, as a failure of consent, as a rejection of the election, and there is a point at which formally cast votes do not suffice for legitimacy. Suppose less than half of those eligible cast ballots; suppose only 30 percent do so. Will it really be a democratically legitimate election if the candidate with the most votes wins? In every formal sense that candidate will be the lawful winner, but in fact his presidency will be fearfully crippled.

A judgment about the legitimacy of a political process cannot be made in a political vacuum. It does seem that the goal of the head counters is to remove politics from the political process. They are pure. They will see no politics, hear no politics, and speak no politics. They would think of people as if they were mere numbers. They want to treat a presidential election as if it were a census. In a census we want to analyze the American population, *to break it down* into just about every conceivable part. Each person is counted as a number in a column, as one in a column titled white or black, or incomes under or above $25,000, or Catholic or Moslem, or married or divorced. In a census our goal is numerical accuracy and recording our diverse and even idiosyncratic characteristics. In a presidential election our goal is the opposite. We want to synthesize, *to bring together* the largest possible support for a national leader and spokesman. When a democratic political process functions properly it builds consensus, it unites.

That is why the most glorious and the most functional moment in our presidential election system is the one in which the loser concedes with a speech that says in essence: the republic still stands; the people have spoken; the consensus has been defined as well as we were able to do it in this election year; we have disagreed and will do so again, but *it's all in the family*.

We have a process in presidential elections, a federal political process, that has actually done this for over two hundred years. Only once, after the election of 1860, did it politically fail—end in civil war. And even then it produced our greatest president, Lincoln, whose resolute vision saved the union of men dedicated to human liberty.

Is there a hidden hand? Does God actually look after children, drunks, and the United States of America? Or is it, perhaps, as I think, a politically functional process? In arithmetic you cannot add apples and oranges; in politics, incredibly, if you have the right process you often can. You can add Catholics and Protestants, whites and blacks, rich and poor, urban and rural, blue collar and white collar into a winning coalition. As Jefferson said, we can add Republicans and Federalists; as Lincoln believed, and in the fullness of time has proved to be true, we can add Southerners and Northerners.

Why does the Electoral College keep on winning? One very good reason is that from a political perspective it produces the right winner. Politics is the architectonic art, the art of the whole not merely of the rule of the greater part, and therefore, the right winner must be defined politically not arithmetically. As a people we believe that the minority have rights, that as fellow citizens they are valuable, that they must be consulted, that their consent if not their enthusiastic approval must be obtained, and that every reasonable effort must be made to include them. As a people we have learned through nation-searing experience that the majority can be wrong, that a majority can oppress a minority. We have learned that the right winner cannot be defined by numbers alone.

Notes

1. David W. Abbott and James P. Levine, *Wrong Winner: The Coming Debacle in the Electoral College* (New York: Praeger, 1991), 33.

Chapter 3

The Federal Principle and the Presidency

Not too long ago while giving the opening lecture in my introductory course in American government, I mentioned the two senators from every state, and a student startled me by stating emphatically, "You're wrong about that." Containing my amusement at his boldness, I replied, "There are many things about which I may be wrong, but that is not one of them. What interests me is: Why do you think I am wrong?" He answered, "It's obvious. New York has nine or ten times as many people as Wyoming; therefore it has many more senators." Said I, "You have come to the right course. You are going to learn a great deal." He did, and one of the things he learned was the federal principle.

What was obvious to this student was that the American democracy is a simple process in which the unlimited, unstructured majority principle is the beginning and the end of democratic legitimacy. If there are 100 Senators and 250,000,000 people, then you simply divide the whole population of the United States by 100 and each Senator represents 2,500,000 people. Or if 500,000 people in Wyoming have one Senator, then 18,000,000 people in New York must have 36 Senators. The only valid principle of representation is one man, one equally weighted vote. Anything that interferes with this is somehow immoral as well as "unconstitutional," for we are a democracy after all.

Here we have a prime case of knowing things "that ain't so." When we speak of the American democracy we are calling our government by a nickname. The proper name for the form of government established by the Constitution is a democratic *federal* republic. Under this form of government, as we all know, we must choose and obey two constitutionally recognized governments, one in Washington and one

31

in each of our respective states. But it means much more than this. It means that the government in Washington is *constructed out of* representatives from people who live in and vote in states. The national government is formed by combining representatives who are chosen by the people in states (the Senate), or in parts of states (the House), or in coalitions of individual states (the presidency), or chosen by representatives who themselves are chosen by the people in the states (the national judiciary).

By rough analogy, a Dean's Council in a college may be composed of one representative elected from each academic department, and each department has its own chairman and by-laws, and its own special mission, interests, and problems. Some of the departments, such as Sociology or English, are large, having ten or more times the faculty and the majors of other departments, such as Philosophy or Geography. Nonetheless, the Dean's Council is composed of a representative from each department, for a college is not made up of unorganized, unattached faculty but of faculty bound to disciplines and based in departments. The national government is composed of representatives from the states because the country is not made up of otherwise unorganized, unattached people but of people bound to obey state governments, people who live in geographically as well as politically defined smaller societies.

Because our republic is federal there are two important constitutional provisions limiting and directing our choices for representatives to the national government. One is the state equality principle; the other is called the federal districting principle. The state equality principle treats the states the way good parents treat children of similar age and rational ability—as having the same rights and rank whether or not they are the same size. One may be taller, or physically stronger, or faster of foot than the other, but their status is the same in the parents' eyes. As constitutionally recognized, self-sustaining societies with governments, the states, for certain purposes, are treated equally. Like cases must be treated alike.

The federal districting principle divides the whole nation into smaller political units and directs that we cast our votes for all of our national elected officers in districts that are either states or parts of states. None of our votes can be combined across state or district lines. A whole can be composed of distinct parts. As the human body is composed of distinct organs, the heart, lungs, and liver, the national body politic is composed of distinct states, distinct because the people within a state or one of its districts must obey a state government that in certain respects is different from all the others.

The federal principle shapes and structures the will of the people by dividing the whole people into smaller parts—into districts that are literally lines on a map. Some of these lines are permanent—the state boundaries. Others change every ten years after the census, when, on the basis of growing or declining population, some states gain seats in the House of Representatives and other states lose seats. The federal principle places a geographic and political mold on the will of the people, giving it distinctive form and distinguishing features. It places a geographical distribution requirement on top of the majority principle. It makes the distribution of the popular votes in national elections as important as the numbers of votes.

The Constitution itself was adopted under the federal principle of state equality. The people in each state acting through special state ratifying conventions determined for themselves if they approved of the Constitution. Approval in nine states was required for adoption, and once nine had ratified it, the Constitution was the law—but *only in those states*. The majority of states could not decide for the minority. Nine states could not legally compel the remaining four to join the Union. Six states with a majority of the whole population could not decide for seven states with a minority of the whole population. Any state that did not ratify would not be part of the United States. Nine states ratified by June 21, 1788, and so the United States was launched. Rhode Island, the last of the original states to agree, didn't ratify and was not part of the Union until almost a year later.

For ratification of the Constitution the states were treated as separate and equal units, and votes could not be added across state lines. The people in Delaware and New Jersey who wanted the Constitution could not combine their votes with those of the people in New York who also wanted it passed and where ratification was a very close thing. Then as now the common interests of people who live under the same state government were recognized.

Today the principle of state equality is recognized in the Senate, where, as my student soon learned, each state has only two senators even if its population is twenty or forty times larger than another state. And that same principle structures the most solemn decision the people can make—amending the Constitution—because each state, regardless of population, is granted one vote in ratifying constitutional amendments, and only the states can ratify amendments either by action of the state legislatures or by special state ratifying conventions.

Since the very first election under the Constitution, the federal districting principle has applied to all national elective offices. As a model of our constitutional system, the presidential election system operates according to both the state equality and the federal districting provisions of the federal principle. The number of electoral votes allotted to each state is the same as the number of representatives each state has in the whole Congress. Each state has two electoral votes to match the state equality principle of the Senate, plus one electoral vote for every representative the state has in the House. And no popular votes in the presidential election can be combined across state lines.

This means that to be successful a presidential candidate must win states. This means the states as political units have an influence on the presidency as well as on the Congress. And because they have an influence on the president, who nominates all the members of the federal bench, as well as on the Senate, which confirms the nominations, the states have an influence on the federal judiciary. The federal principle is the fulcrum, the fixed support, for the whole national government and for the Constitution. It is the base on which all three branches of government turn. Applying the principle to the presidency establishes balance in the arrangement of the three branches.

Since the federal principle places limits on the will of the national majority, since it places geographic barriers (the state and district lines) around our votes thus adding a distribution requirement to the simple majority principle, why is it in the Constitution?

Balancing the Local and National Interests

First, in a large, heterogeneous, continental republic there must be a balance between the local and the national interests so that the legitimate interests of the people in one part of the whole nation are not carelessly neglected or unnecessarily sacrificed. There must be a way to protect the interests of the local minority.

This was the kind of problem the American colonists faced with the British Parliament. The battle cry of our revolution—Taxation Without Representation Is Tyranny!—would seem to suggest that the British could have avoided the American revolution by giving the colonists seats in Parliament on the basis of one man, one vote. Not so. Representation and majority rule don't suffice because, without some mechanism like our federal principle, the local interest will lose. Even if the British had allowed the American colonists to be represented in Parliament, the Americans would have been outvoted on the issue of taxes on the colonies. They also could have been outvoted on everything else that was vital to the colonists, thus making them second class citizens. So much for the practical utility of representation alone.

The problem was that the American colonists lived in geographically distinct societies that had their own local problems, local interests, and local governments. They lived in societies that were parts of a larger society, the mother country, yet their interests as members of these smaller societies, the colonies, could not be protected by the simple majority representation principle of one man, one vote.

Human nature being what it is, we tend to identify the national interest with our own interest, and the unstructured majority will do the same and disregard a legitimate local interest. If the national policy makers didn't represent the opinions of the people as state citizens but rather represented the opinions of people as expressed in national opinion polls, what a selfish majority might choose to call "the national interest" could easily destroy a legitimate local interest. Example: We've got to do something with nuclear waste, and none of us want it in our state. Not in my back yard! So let's send it all to Utah and turn Utah into our national nuclear dump.

It may be in our national interest to close some military bases in certain places in order to cut the national deficit, but since such a closure could destroy the economy of the area around the base, some form of national assistance, perhaps in job training or development loans, must accompany the closure decision. A part of the people should not bear the burden of the whole if there is any way to avoid it. Creating a national government that is federal, that is made up of representatives who speak for the opinions and interests of people in separate states, means that the national government will be sensitive to local needs and local rights will be recognized.

The president is a major player in the national government. Therefore, it is imperative that he also be responsive to state viewpoints. Because of the electoral vote system he is. The president cannot simply win a majority of the popular vote. He must win a majority of the electoral vote, and that means he must win states. To do this he must be sensitive to the interests of the states. The electoral vote system requires that successful candidates for the presidency seek consensus by building the broadest possible coalition of local interests.

Defining the National Interest

The second reason why the federal system is in the Constitution is that the national interest must be defined by creating *political* majorities. Here I use the term "political" in its original Greek sense of *polis* membership—of common citizenship in a permanent, organized, self-governing society. Political majorities, in this sense, are public, open to all members of the society, not private, not closed to those who do not share the same race, ethnic ancestry, religion, or gender. In a large, heterogeneous republic political majorities must be broadly inclusive alliances of political minorities that can compromise. The states are such political minorities, and they are the building blocks of the political majorities in the United States.

Basing representation on common state citizenship prevents private minorities from uniting their votes across state lines, makes it necessary for them to compromise at the state level with many and various other interests in order to form state and local majorities. Thus it nurtures consensus. To illustrate: the professional football players union is made up of representatives elected by the teams, not representatives elected by players defined by position. The quarterbacks from all the teams do not band together and send their own representatives to the union, nor do the running backs or the defensive backs send their own separate spokesmen. Team representation promotes team cohesion and morale and creates a union that will protect and promote the game of football by keeping the interests of the various positions in balance. Quarterbacks and defensive backs have very different and in fact incompatible position-based interests, interests that if not reconciled will destroy a team and the game. Furthermore, there are a lot more defensive backs on a team than quarterbacks. A system that bases representation on teams rather than player positions forces players to compromise and emphasizes their common interests as team members. It shifts their focus from their private interests to the interests of all football players.

The nonfederal arithmetical majority simply isn't adequate to define the national interest because of the fact of private group formation, because a number of voters can unite on the basis of some private special interest in order to gang up on other folk. James Madison called such groups factions. If human beings didn't form such private groups then the arithmetical majority principle might be enough, but the fact is they do. And because they do it is necessary to take some other steps so that government isn't simply another name for a band of robbers—a band of robbers who use votes, rather than guns and knives, to prey upon their fellow citizens. In *Federalist* 51, Madison tells us that it is of great importance "to guard one part of society against the injustice of the other part." To do this he recommends "a proper federal system"—a society composed of societies.

A society of societies is not a confederation, not a loose league of fully sovereign states for mutual defense. Rather it is a true community with a supreme national government. Our national motto reflects the federal principle: E Pluribus Unum—out of many, one—out of many societies, one society, one people. The name of our nation also emphasizes its federal nature: The United States of America, not simply America, not the American States. It is neither a unitary system nor a confederation.

How does "a proper federal system" prevent one part of society from mugging another? The answer is the new science of faction, which uses private special interests to check and control each other. Since this new science employs faction it must officially recognize and promote only the least dangerous kinds of factions. When we need to employ animals we choose relatively docile ones like horses and oxen. We do not choose lions and tigers and bears. And it must find a way to tame or contain the most dangerous kinds of factions.

The kinds of factions that can be most safely recognized and represented in the national government are the heterogeneous, small political minorities we call states. The citizens of the states share a relatively safe common interest—the managing of the resources of a community. They are heterogeneous because to be viable they must contain a wide variety of economic interests. There must be farmers, plumbers, electricians, garbage collectors, teachers, doctors, manufacturers, bus drivers, police officers, and butchers and bakers and candlestick makers. The states as states can be self-supporting in terms of daily life. They are small republics. They are life-sustaining societies.

Because the people of a state live together and share the same roads, parks, schools, natural resources, climate, local economy, taxes, laws, and government, they have common interests that should be represented. The people who live in them have interests that, in terms of their day-to-day lives, are at least as important and probably more important than the characteristics they share with people in other states, such as religion, race, ethnic ancestry, or gender. The people who live in Maine share interests and problems that are different from the people in New Mexico. And the people in New Mexico share interests and problems that are different from the people in Wisconsin or the people in Tennessee. Thus the people in each state form what from the national point of view is a political minority that is in itself heterogeneous and can compromise.

Dangerous factions are homogeneous, monolithic, all-of-one-kind factions. They are based on the accidents of clan membership rather than the fraternity of self-selected state citizenship. They are lions and tigers and bears. Only foolish founders would choose to recognize and directly represent such dangerous competitors. They would devour each other and the country in civil strife and civil war.

The federal principle, because it does not recognize and does not directly represent these kinds of factions at the national level in the form of a black party and a white party, a Christian party and a Moslem and a Jewish party, an Anglo and an Hispanic and an Asian ancestry party, isolates and insulates the nation to some degree from the insidious effects of their competition. It reminds the members of these private groups that they live together, that they have a common interest based on their state citizenship—a civic interest that can transcend their private interest. It forces such factions to compromise with each other at the state and state district levels in order to elect representatives to the national government. All politics, to this degree, is local—the society composed of societies. And to the extent that the states are neither required *nor permitted* to draw district lines solely on the basis of whether people belong to private exclusive groups— blacks, Hispanics, Christians, or even women—all politics will be public and open to all citizens.

The federal principle keeps dangerous factions within bounds by penning them up in multiple small societies. If dangerous factions cannot directly combine their votes across state lines, their destructive potential is reduced. If they are confined within the boundaries of a state, the necessity to compromise in order to achieve national representation can instill moderation. Like the quarterbacks and de- fensive backs who share the same representation in the players union, the various private factions must share the same representation in the national government. In this way private factional interests are converted into public minorities.

The national interest is defined by the representatives of these *public* minorities. It is worked out in a process of consultation, negotiation, and compromise among all of our elected national representatives, a process that creates a political majority. Using a federal districting process rather than an all-national head count to define the national interest means that the definition will come closer to the common good.

Because the president has a powerful voice in defining the national interest, it is just as important for the presidency to be subjected to the moderating influence of the federal system as it is the Congress. It may be even more important since the presidency is controlled by one man. Congress is subject to an internal control because it is a plural and bicameral body. The essential unity of the presidency makes it all the more necessary that the president should not be the voice of a private faction.

The Federal Principle and the Separation of Powers

The third reason for the federal system is the fact that the separation of powers and the federal principle work in tandem. The separation of powers cannot protect minorities without the federal principle. The separation of powers (the division of the national government into three separate branches, one of which is divided further into two chambers) was designed to prevent the government from oppressing the people by making the various branches of government rivals, checking and balancing each other. Without the federal principle, however, the separation of powers will fail.

Most people ignore the importance of the federal principle, especially in presidential elections, thinking that with the separation of powers firmly placed in the Constitution the only thing necessary to fill the office of president is universal suffrage and an all-national head count. Voting for representatives, of course, is necessary, for it is the way of registering the ongoing consent of the people and of keeping the representatives faithful. But faithful to whom? The answer is to the majority or the plurality of the people. Many of us can quote Jefferson: "The will of the majority is in all cases to prevail."

There would be no problem with this answer if everyone in this country had the same interests, or if the effects of governmental decisions were the same on all. Neither of these conditions can be met. We are a heterogeneous people, and the actions of government invariably have unequal effects because of the first law of politics and economics—TANSTAAFL—the acronym for "there ain't no such thing as a free lunch." In order to provide benefits the government must also create burdens, and the burdens are not the same for all. The most obvious example is a draft law where the burden falls on young men and now perhaps young women, and the benefit falls to children, the middle aged, and the old. Another obvious example is in tax policy, which makes some people taxpayers, people who pay in more than they get back in benefits, and makes other people tax consumers, people who get back in benefits more than they pay in taxes. An examination of just about any governmental policy will reveal that the actions of government produce unequal effects.

And who will get the benefits? They will go to the supporters of those who win the elections, to the party that controls the government. To the victors go the spoils. This poses a severe problem for, while there is no form of government whose policies do not produce unequal effects, if you would avoid continual civil strife and even revolution care must be taken that the burdens be reasonable. The second part of Jefferson's statement is the crucial part for while the will of the majority must prevail "that will to be rightful, must be reasonable."

Suffrage alone will not suffice to create reasonable majorities because suffrage keeps the representatives faithful to those who voted for them. But this means that the representatives can be faithful to an unjust master, to a majority that would act like a band of robbers. Add the separation of powers to suffrage and there still isn't enough to create reasonable majorities because all three branches of the national government can be captured and controlled by the same party. A party bridges the gaps created by the separation of powers. It is a unifying device, and a necessary one at that. But one can have too much of a good thing. In this case too much means a homogeneous, disciplined party whose members share identical interests and principles and who march in lockstep supporting the party line.

However, if we add to the foregoing "a proper federal system," one party will not fully control the whole government, at least not one whose members agree on all points. Even when the same party gains control over the presidency as well as both chambers of Congress we will have a presidential party and a congressional party or rather two congressional parties—one for each chamber. And since the members of the House and the Senate do not owe their seats to a national party but rather to state and local parties, the members have the motive to vote against their national parties on occasion. Under our federal system, the average member of Congress votes against his congressional party's position a third of the time. And yet the national party leaders cannot deny the party label to fellow partisans who vote against the party in Congress.

In one sense, except in presidential elections, the notion of national parties is a myth of the media. Because of the federal principle, what we call a national political party is actually a loose combination of fifty state parties, and so party label is a kind of ragged patch that hides different regional and local interests and even principles. The Democratic Party in New York is not identical to the Democratic Party in Nebraska or the Democratic Party in Georgia. And party members elected from these states will not always agree and vote together or support the president of their party. Some if not many of them will have out-polled the president of their party in their own states or districts and may correctly conclude that it would be political suicide to support certain of the president's policies.

This means that although one party may nominally control the government, the separation of powers will still work. A president whose party controls Congress will not always or necessarily be able to get his programs passed or passed without major revisions and compromises with members of his own party. He may not be able to get his programs passed without some support from members of the minority party in Congress. Further, the president may not agree with all the policies passed by a Congress controlled by his own party and therefore will choose to exercise his veto. Adding in the federal principle means that although the president, the senators, and the congressmen all have districted state constituencies, they represent somewhat different interests and therefore are competitors who must compromise.

The will of the majority to be rightful must be reasonable. Reasonable majorities are created by a process of "opposite and rival interests," by representatives who have both the means and the motives to check each other, and the federal principle structures the popular vote in such a way as to supply a goodly part of the motives. Why does the Electoral College keep on winning? It is a major support of the federal system, which balances the national and the local interests, gives us a moderate, inclusive, political definition of the national interest, supports the separation of powers, and thereby prevents majority tyranny.

Chapter 4

Closing the College

On the Monday following the second Wednesday of December 1992, the host of a national radio talk show began his program on the Electoral College by stating dramatically: "Today is the most important news day of the year!" An amusing bit of irony, a bit of teasing, for that was the day the electors met to cast the official votes that made Bill Clinton president. Of course, it wasn't the most important news day of the year nor was it even the most important news of the day. There were no three-inch headlines proclaiming Clinton the winner; those headlines were published on November 4, 1992, the day after the general election. News of the meeting of the electors was buried, appropriately, on the fourth page or used as fill in the sports section.

The meeting of the electors was a pro forma ritual—a legal technicality. The people knew that the real election had already taken place, and the people were right. For all practical purposes the electoral votes had already been cast by the media as they reported the state-by-state popular vote tallies, and when Clinton had achieved 270 electoral votes they proclaimed him the winner. The office of elector, *but not the electoral vote system itself*, is obsolete and made so by modern communications.

Why Was the Electoral College Created?

One of the many myths about the College perpetuated by careless or misinformed commentators is that the framers distrusted the people—that the framers were undemocratic and thus decided to give the choice of president to an elite, the electors. The fact is that the Electoral

College was promoted by the very members of the Constitutional Convention who trusted the people, by James Wilson and James Madison. According to the Constitution, the state legislatures decide how the electors will be chosen. The leading members of the Convention who supported this provision hoped and believed that it would lead the states to choose popular elections for electors. They were soon proven right, and by 1836 all the states but one had popular elections for presidential electors.

To some extent the myth arises because of the human tendency "to commit anachronism"—to impose the conditions of the present on the past. At the time of the framing of the Constitution there was no national television, no national radio, not even national newspapers. Communication was slow and required long, laborious journeys on horseback. The framers wanted a president who could unite the nation, but they feared, with good reason, that the people, not knowing about the leading men in other states, would choose only a "favorite son"—their own state's native son. The people in Connecticut probably would not know about the talented men from Virginia or Georgia and the reverse.

The men who would be chosen as electors would be men who were actively engaged in political life, who would be in continual correspondence with their counterparts in other states, and therefore, would be more familiar with the national pool of candidates. To assure that they would consider candidates who weren't simply hometown boys, originally the electors were required to cast two votes for president, not just one, and at least one of these two votes had to be cast for a person outside of their own state.

Given the communications conditions of the time this was neither unreasonable nor undemocratic. Practically, it gave the electors a kind of mechanical nominating function as well as an electing function. It was no more undemocratic than our current process of choosing members of the national judiciary or the members of the president's cabinet. We do not vote for these national officers, our elected representatives do. The presumption is that these elected representatives know us, they know the kind of men we want, they know far more than we about the pool of candidates for such jobs, and thus they know who is qualified to serve. How many of us could name five qualified candidates for the Supreme Court or for secretary of defense?

In parliamentary systems the chief executive is chosen by the members of the legislature, not by a vote of the people, and most of the democratic nations of the world have parliamentary systems. Same principle. However, the framers rejected a parliamentary system in favor of the separation of powers. The president must not be chosen by Congress except as a last resort to fill the office because that would destroy his independence. The framers decided they needed another body to do the executive selecting job that the legislature does in parliamentary systems, and they considered it so important to keep Congress out of the ordinary process of selecting the president that they prohibited any member of Congress or any "Person holding an Office of Trust or Profit under the United States" from serving as an elector. They wanted an independent president, so he was not to be chosen by any continuous body that could undermine his independence or seek to cut a secret deal with any candidate. The College exists for only one day and never meets as a unified body. Each state's electors meet separately in their own state capital and send their votes to Congress separately.

Today we all have instant and easy access to the national media, which often provides us with more information about the pool of presidential candidates than we want to know. Today we have the party system to perform the important task of nominating candidates. Today we know who won the election before the College meets. Today all the states have popular elections to determine how their electoral votes will be cast. For all practical purposes the people do choose the president, and to say that they don't is a mere technicality—a quibble. The electors once had a real function; now they have none. For this reason the most widely acceptable plan for reforming the system of presidential elections is the automatic plan, which abolishes the office of elector but retains the electoral votes.

The Automatic Plan

The meeting of the College may be mere ritual, but ritual and ceremony often are important in the life of a nation; they can serve to unify a people, to maintain continuity and to connect the generations. We should have good reasons for abandoning ritual and ceremony, and in this case we have. We can and should abolish the office of elector, *but not the electoral votes*. The electoral votes can be cast automatically; we don't need living electors to do it. There are several problems that would be solved by so doing.

To do this would clear up misconceptions about the electoral vote system and perhaps even silence some of the quibblers. It would also solve the so-called problem of the faithless elector. Though pledged to support a certain candidate and elected on the basis of that pledge, the faithless elector casts his vote for some other person. The fear is that a faithless elector or several of them could steal the election and subvert the will of the people. This has not ever happened or even come close to happening. There have been over 16,000 electoral votes cast in our history, and only eight have been miscast. None of these eight faithless electors changed the outcome of the election or intended to do so. They simply misused their office to make a personal or political statement.

Twenty-four states bind their electors and five of them provide penalties for violating a pledge. Nonetheless it is possible for an elector even from these states to do so, and there is no good reason for taking even this slight risk. The Supreme Court has not ruled on the question of whether or not the electors can be compelled to honor their pledges. By eliminating the office of elector, the automatic plan would solve this problem.

It would also go a long way toward solving others that arise because of the possibility of the death or resignation of a presidential candidate. In such a case there is both a gap and an inconsistency in the process that could be alleviated if the office of elector were abolished. To understand this we have to imagine several different scenarios, and to make it simple let's just deal with the possibility of death.

First, suppose a presidential candidate dies before the general election. The national committee of the party then will choose a new candidate, and no doubt they would choose their candidate for the vice presidency. After all if their victorious presidential candidate had died after the inauguration, the vice president would succeed. Sad as it is to say, the main and only constitutional duty of the vice president (other than serving as the official president of the Senate, where he has no vote except in a tie) is to be alive if the president dies. There is precedent for the choice falling to the national committee of the party. In 1972, when the Democratic Party's candidate for vice president, Senator Thomas Eagleton, withdrew after the party convention, the party's national committee named Sargent Shriver as his replacement. There's no problem with this scenario, for the people have not yet voted.

Suppose instead that the death of the winning presidential candidate happened after the general election in November and before the meeting of the Electoral College on the first Monday following the second Wednesday in December. The problem is that there is no statutory provision to cover this. Most people presume that the national party would choose the replacement for whom their electors would vote. And they presume the replacement would be the vice presidential running mate. Presumption is not enough; the people have already voted.

Someone would have to replace the deceased candidate because the electors are to vote for a person. There is real doubt that a deceased candidate is a person under the law. In the election of 1872, Horace Greeley, the Democratic candidate who won the vote in six states, died before the meeting of the College. Most of his electors voted for other persons, and Congress officially counted those votes. However, three Georgia electors voted for Greeley. Congress refused to count these votes on the ground that they were not cast for a person. Since Greeley had not won the general election, the issue was legal and technical rather than immediately political, but it serves as a precedent.

Congress could fill this gap with a statute authorizing the national committee of the party that has won in November to name the replacement. This would fill the gap, but it does not actually suffice because it would be possible, though politically improbable, for the national committee to name someone other than the vice presidential running mate as the replacement. However, if by constitutional amendment we abolished the office of elector and awarded the electoral votes automatically, this gap would be closed and the running mate of the deceased victorious presidential candidate would succeed.

To understand the inconsistency imagine and compare the following two scenarios. Suppose the death of the winning presidential candidate happens after January 6th (the date set by statute for Congress to count the electoral votes) and before the January 20th inauguration. No problem so far. The Twentieth Amendment takes effect and the vice president-elect succeeds to the presidency.

But suppose, instead, that the death of the winning presidential candidate occurs after the Electoral College meets in December and before Congress counts the electoral votes on January 6th. The votes were cast for a living person. Can they be counted for a dead one? If an elector cannot cast a vote for a dead "person," surely Congress cannot count votes for a dead "person." The Twelfth Amendment says: "The *person* having the greatest number of votes for President, shall be the President, if such number be a majority of the whole number of Electors appointed." (Emphasis added).

Now we have an inconsistency and a problem, for, in this scenario, the contingency election of the Twelfth Amendment comes into play. This means that the House of Representatives must choose among the top three candidates who won electoral votes for president. For president, not for vice president! The deceased winner's running mate, the winning vice presidential candidate, would not become president nor would he be one of the candidates from whom the House would choose the president. Instead, one of the losing presidential candidates would win the presidency! In the first scenario we have one result, in the second quite another. Whether the deceased victorious candidate's running mate becomes president turns on when the death occurs. If it occurs on January 7th, the vice president-elect becomes president, but if it occurs two days earlier he does not. He is still vice president but will serve a president of another party, a party that lost the election. This is the kind of nightmare that could tempt an assassin. We have been fortunate that no winning candidate has died between the meeting of the College and the congressional counting of the votes.

Congress may be able to fill the gap with statutory law, but it cannot resolve the inconsistency with statutory law short of a contingency election in the House of Representatives. If no electoral votes can be counted for a deceased "person," the death of the candidate for whom a majority of electoral votes were cast—but not counted—triggers the House contingency election. Under Section 4 of the Twentieth Amendment, Congress may "provide for the case of the death of any of the persons from whom the House of Representatives may choose a President whenever the right of choice shall have developed upon them." Congress has not as yet done so. Presumably, by prior stat- ute—before the tragic event occurred—Congress could declare that the vice president-elect be one of the candidates from whom the House would choose the new president. However, this would not guarantee that the vice president-elect succeeded for he would be only one of two or at most three candidates under House consideration. And the House contingency procedure is highly problematic in itself. It could become a media circus and a national ordeal.

Here is a problem that can be solved by an amendment abolishing the office of elector with the further provision that if a presidential candidate dies or resigns before the January counting of the electoral votes, his electoral votes shall automatically fall to his vice presidential running mate. The vice presidential vacancy would subsequently be filled under the provisions of the Twenty-fifth Amendment. And re- member such an amendment would also solve the problems of faith- less electors.

So why haven't we fired the fellows? Some think that the benefits gained are too small to justify the effort to pass a constitutional amendment. Others think that the proposal falls far short of the reforms they believe desirable. Most of these people want to abolish the electoral vote system as well as the office of elector, and, while they would be happy to see the electors eliminated, they believe that adoption of the automatic plan would reduce the momentum for more radical change. Still others, those who oppose radical changes, fear that any serious effort to adopt the automatic plan would open Pandora's box—create an opening for those who oppose the federal principle in presidential elections. They warn that any movement to change the presidential election process cannot be limited to firing the electors.

Further, most proposed versions of the automatic plan contain an additional provision that would constitutionalize the winner-take-all system of allocating electoral votes currently practiced by all but two of the states. Simply, it would declare that the candidate who received the greatest number of popular votes in a given state shall be entitled to all of that state's electoral votes. According to its advocates, to place this long practiced provision in the Constitution would secure the federal principle in presidential elections, support the two-party system, and make the general election the only election, thereby avoiding the problems of contingency elections. From the perspective of the radical reformers, however, this would make a bad situation worse. They think it is bad enough that most states use the winner-take-all rule in allocating their electoral votes, and that it would be worse to take away the states' option of allocating proportionally the electoral votes among candidates. And of course, some state legislatures, jealous of their prerogatives under the Constitution, would oppose this as a reduction of state power. And so the Electoral College keeps on winning.

Chapter 5

Beating the Alternatives

Grandmother used to say, "There's always another way to skin a rat. It just depends on what you want to do with the rat or the skin." Years later I learned this homely bit of advice on choosing among alternatives had another name—cost-benefit analysis. The first step in this method is to clearly define your goal, then you assess the costs and benefits of each alternative, and finally you choose the alternative that attains the greatest benefit at the least cost.

There are alternatives to the current method of selecting the president, and we must weigh the costs and benefits of each method. But since the president is merely one player in a larger constitutional system, before we can define the goals of a presidential selection process, we must be clear about the larger process. The head coach must have an understanding of the game of football and the roles of all the players before he can decide who his quarterback will be. He cannot decide on the quarterback in the abstract as though the quarterback were the only player on the field. He must consider the role of the quarterback in relation to all of the other playing positions. To do this in presidential selection means we must take the perspective of the framers of the Constitution.

Assume you are a framer and that because your goal is human liberty you have already decided on a republic rather than a simple democracy because a republic is ruled by laws and not by men. And in a republic the people do not vote directly on all the laws because there are representatives to refine and enlarge the public view and thereby build consensus. To make a long story short, assume, further, that you have already decided on a large, federal republic with separation of powers and for the same reasons. Now you have the task of deciding how to select the president, and you must define your method of presidential selection in light of the whole governing process. Let's make a list. First, your selection method must fill the office. This is an office that can never go empty, for, under the separation of powers, the president is the Head of State and the Commander in Chief—he is the only person who speaks for the whole nation, and the only person who has supreme command over the nation's defense forces.

A little thought on the latter, especially in the modern world of weapons technology, leads to the conclusion that a second requirement must be a swift, sure, clean, and clear decision. There must never be doubt about who the president is, and an extended period of uncertainty about who the president will be not only fosters intrigue and tempts foreign enemies, but also shortens the time for the orderly transfer of power. A system that makes the general election the only election is to be preferred over one that produces frequent runoffs or other forms of contingency elections. In an ideal world we would, of course, want the best choice no matter how long it took, but in the real world some decision is often better than no decision. If you are in a foxhole being shelled it is better to have a decision—advance or retreat. What you don't want, while the shells are falling on you, is a committee debating about who has the authority to decide.

Disputed elections are an equally serious problem, and so a third requirement is that the system must reduce the possibility of fraud and thus of national recounts, elections tied up in the courts, and presidencies crippled by suspicion of fraud. No electoral system can totally prevent fraud, but a system that reduces its effects by boxing it off, quarantining it so that it does not infect the whole vote, is to be preferred.

Fourth, under the separation of powers, the president must be independent so he can be an energetic leader and perform his checking and balancing function. Therefore, he must not be chosen by Congress except as a last resort to fill the office. If he is chosen by Congress, Congress will control him. It can set conditions on his decisions in exchange for the office, especially if Congress is given the power to remove him from office if he betrays his trust (and some elected body must be given such a power if liberty is to be preserved). If Congress chooses the president, candidates will court its members rather than the people, and then who will protect the people from the Congress, which can develop a separate, elite interest? Anyone who is aware of the fact that Congress once exempted itself from many of the laws it required the rest of us to obey knows law-makers can create privileges for themselves at the expense of the people. Any system that excludes

Congress from the process, except in extraordinary circumstances, is desirable if the separation of powers principle is correct.

Fifth, the method of selection must produce a president who can govern. In this country and in this day and age that means that the people must choose. The president must have the support of at least a plurality and, better, a majority of the people. Our republic is a democratic one after all. And since this is a heterogeneous, continental nation, it is more important that popular support be broad than deep—popular votes for the president must be widely distributed rather than concentrated in one section of the country. The people's choice, the right winner, must represent the nation in its diversity. Therefore, some device must be adopted to structure and shape the popular majority or plurality, to give candidates a motive to build a broad cross-sectional base of support.

Sixth, the method of selection must preserve the federal system and thus balance of power between the president and the Congress, and between the national and local interests. This means that the method of presidential selection should be compatible with the method of selecting the Congress—the base of both institutions should be recognized as the same. As Congress has a federal base, so should the presidency. If the method of selection allows the president to claim a more "authentic" mandate than that of the Congress, his power and prestige will be enhanced at the expense of Congress and at the expense of local interests. We want an energetic presidency, not an imperial one. As the method of selection must not produce a dwarf so it must not produce a giant, a Caesar.

Seventh, a presidential selection system should produce moderate winners, winners who are at least tolerable to the losing side. The election of the president must not be perceived as a zero-sum game where one side wins everything important and the other side loses everything important. The losing side may be disappointed and even disgusted, but it must not be totally alienated. This means the selection method must favor a two-party system rather than a multi-party system. A two-party system promotes coalition building, develops consensus, and produces moderate rather than extremist or single-issue candidates. Multi-party systems do the opposite and as a result are notoriously unstable.

In a two-way race one candidate will achieve a majority. A three-way or a four-way race can splinter the vote, with no candidate achieving a majority, and while there will be a plurality it could be a mere 26 to 30 percent of the popular vote. That is not enough to govern, and so a multi-party system will require frequent runoffs and probably frequent recounts to determine which two candidates will be in the runoff. To avoid this and to gain the benefits of moderation and consensus building, the presidential selection system must promote a two-party system, but not prohibit third parties. It is possible that a third party will become one of the two major parties as happened in the 1850s, when the Republicans replaced the Whigs. But even when it does not, a third party does perform the function of keeping the two major parties on a consensus-building track by drawing their attention to those who are disaffected. Third parties also are often the sources of new ideas.

To summarize, the method of presidential selection should:

1. Fill the office
2. Produce a swift, sure, clean, and clear decision
3. Reduce the premium on fraud
4. Produce a president who is independent thereby supporting the separation of powers
5. Produce a president who can govern because of sufficient popular support
6. Preserve the federal system
7. Produce moderate winners who are tolerable to the losers

This is a tall order. The goals of presidential selection are multiple and complex, and so it should not be surprising if the process that achieves these goals is complex. The current system fulfills or comes very close to fulfilling them all. The Automatic Plan would change nothing substantive but only convert an election that is direct in practice into one that is direct as a matter of constitutional law. How do the other reform plans measure up?

The Direct Election Plan

Under the direct election plan every vote would be cast and counted as if there were one national ballot box. To win, a candidate would have to poll an all-national plurality of at least 40 percent. At first it strikes one as an elegant solution. It's uncomplicated, seems to be really democratic, and appears to solve possible problems in the existing system, such as the possibility of a runner-up president. I confess that when I first heard of it more than thirty years ago, I was ready to sign on—until I analyzed this plan and discovered not only that it defeats five of the seven goals listed above, it also would deform our Constitution. Of the above goals, the only two it would achieve are to fill the office and produce a president who is independent. Thus its costs are great and, from a constitutional perspective, very serious— the most serious is the implicit attack on the federal principle.

Its supporters call their plan direct election. It should be called direct nonfederal election. The current system is, in fact if not in law, a direct election and a federal one. Since there is widespread support for an automatic plan that would abolish the office of elector but not the electoral votes, and since the proponents of the direct election plan reject the automatic plan, it should be clear that the essence of their proposal is that it is nonfederal.

The proponents of direct nonfederal election do want to fill the office swiftly and surely, cleanly and clearly. However, it is more likely to do the opposite. Removing the win-states requirement of the current federal system will weaken the two-party system and increase the number of candidates. Now, third-party candidates who cannot poll a plurality in a single state cannot trigger a contingency election. Under direct nonfederal election they could do so because the more candidates the less likely it is that any candidate will poll a national majority. If the advocates of direct nonfederal election stuck with a majority requirement for victory, nearly every general election would be turned into a national primary followed by a runoff election. The undesirability of runoffs has led them to reduce their victory requirement to a 40 percent, popular vote plurality. There is nothing magical about the 40 percent figure—42 or 45 percent would not make much difference. While 40 percent plus pluralities have been the rule (with the exception of Lincoln, who was not on the ballot in ten states), if you abolish the federal principle in presidential elections, everything can change. Many of the proponents of the direct nonfederal election with a 40 percent plurality rule assume that they can make such a major change in the rules without changing the way the game is played and without changing the nature of the winning team. That is nonsense.

The fact that these rather rigid majoritarians are willing to compromise their principle to preclude runoffs is strong evidence against runoff elections. This compromise is a real sacrifice on their part because logically their principle of legitimacy is arithmetic, and in arithmetic a majority is 50 percent plus one; thus any limit on or deviation from this is undemocratic. Unless you hold a runoff election there is no accurate way to assert that the candidate who won a plurality has or would have the support of a majority. The runner-up in a general election might very well be the choice of a majority in a runoff election. Multi-candidate races are often produced by splits in one party, splits that might be healed in a runoff. In 1912, Wilson won the presidency with 41.8 percent of the popular vote as a result of a Republican split between Teddy Roosevelt and Taft. If there had been a runoff, the Republicans could have united, and runner-up Roosevelt could have defeated Wilson.

The sad thing here is that their sacrifice is for naught. Even with their 40 percent plurality victory requirement, runoffs will be the rule and not the exception. This is because politics is not arithmetic, and a second-chance psychology will infect both candidates and voters. It is the very existence of a popular vote runoff, a second chance provision, that tempts more candidates to enter and voters to cast what they would otherwise consider to be a protest vote—a "send them a message" vote. The Perot candidacy, in 1992, created a panic that no candidate would win a majority of the electoral vote even though the current system has never triggered a contingency election because it magnifies the plurality winner's margin of victory in the electoral votes.

If the 40 percent runoff rule in an all-national election had been the law in 1992, a runoff would have been very likely. Perot would not have withdrawn temporarily because he could win something by triggering a popular vote runoff even if he himself wasn't in the runoff. He could offer his support to one of the two runoff candidates in return for a 50 cent increase in the gasoline tax to pay off the deficit, or for a protectionist trade treaty, or for a cabinet position. Now with Perot in, put yourself in the shoes of other potential candidates and consider what you would do if the law allowed a popular vote runoff. Jerry Brown fought for the Democratic nomination all the way to the national convention, and Pat Buchanan was just as adamant on the Republican side. Without the federal principle and the magnifier effect of the state unit rule, every additional candidacy would put a 40 percent plurality in doubt. Even without Brown and Buchanan, Clinton won just 43 percent of the popular vote. Brown and Buchanan are likely, and why not Jack Kemp and Mario Cuomo, and Jesse Jackson? They could be followed by the feminist candidate, the Hispanic candidate, the moral majority candidate, the environmental candidate, the gay rights candidate, the military candidate. The general election could be turned into a multi-issue public policy opinion poll. As one wag who considered this kind of scenario put it, on the day before the election, the *New York Times* would have to print a five-page supplement just to identify all the candidates.

As if making runoffs the rule were not enough, the splintering of the vote works against the moderate candidates and works to the advantage of the immoderate, extreme candidates. It does this because the middle is where the inclusive coalitions can be built. By undermining coalition building prior to the general election, a runoff fragments the middle, not the extremes; the extremes are rarely fragmented—fanatics have solidarity. Coalition building seeks to spotlight most people's second choice, which is a satisfactory and inclusive choice.

To illustrate very roughly, suppose we all had to cast one vote for the kind of ice cream all Americans would be served. Our choices are: chocolate, strawberry, vanilla, French vanilla, chocolate chip, chocolate mint chip, fudge ripple, pumpkin, and chicken ripple. Probably one of the first three would be the second choice of most people, if they could not have their first choice. It strikes us as most unlikely that pumpkin or chicken ripple would be most people's third, or even sixth choice. But what happens in this multi-choice vote is that the split in the middle, among the flavors most people would choose second or even third, relatively elevates pumpkin and even chicken ripple. It makes them appear to be contenders with French vanilla and chocolate chip even though pumpkin and chicken ripple are unusual preferences. (People who prefer chicken ripple are not likely to compromise with those who like chocolate or vanilla.) It is even possible, given the large number of tolerable preferences, that vanilla won't be in the runoff. With the division of the middle, pumpkin may poll nearly as much support as French vanilla or chocolate chip, and therefore will have more impact and influence than it actually deserves. The point is that most people's second choice, the choice that has the greatest chance of success in governing, may be out of the runoff, and, if it is in the runoff, may have to compromise with the group that has the least real claim to popular support.

But would the people really scatter their votes among so many candidates? The answer of second-chance psychology is yes. Americans have great expectations for the presidency, perhaps too great. (They want a hero, but heroes are not always among us, and real heroes often won't run for the presidency. If they will, sadly, we don't always recognize them.) This may be one explanation for the popularity of a lecture I give in my introductory course titled: "Why Out of a Nation of More than Two Hundred Million People Do We

Have to Choose between These Two Jerks for President?'' Students
who are not even enrolled in the course show up for that lecture.

With that in mind, let's take the voter's perspective. Neither of the
two major parties is running a hero. The fact is that they are both
jerks. Oh yes, they have their groupies, but the rest of us who are
sober know they are both jerks. What to do? If you know that one of
them will win under the present system, if you know you will not have
a second chance to vote (as most Americans do know intuitively even
though they cannot fully explain why) then you choose the lesser jerk.
Now let's change the rules so that it's doubtful that anyone will win a
required 40 percent plurality. Now you can blow off steam by voting
for a third-party candidate, or by voting for a single-issue candidate,
register your opinion on abortion or gay rights. They're all jerks, but
you can send a message to the two major parties by casting a protest
vote for one of the other jerks, and you are reasonably assured of
having a chance to vote again in the runoff, where you still can vote
for the lesser jerk. The second-chance psychology encourages multiple
candidates and parties; it highlights our differences rather than builds
consensus.

Not only will the 40 percent rule make the decision less swift and
sure, not only will it make our candidates and politics less moderate,
it will also make the decision less clean and clear because in abolishing
the electoral votes, it also removes the quarantine on fraud and
recounts. Since, under the current system, popular votes cannot be
added across state lines, charges of fraud and demands for a recount
in one state do not lead to demands for recounts and court challenges
in all states. The outcome in Maine will not change the outcome in
Texas or the reverse. In fact, even when there is question about the
tabulation in one state there will not necessarily be a demand for a
recount or a challenge in the courts. The only time a runner-up will
refuse to concede, demand recounts and initiate court challenges is if
the electoral votes of a questionable state or a few states will give him
the victory. The electoral vote system isolates instances of fraud and
prevents the contamination of the whole.

However, if we adopt the direct nonfederal election plan, a recount
of every ballot box in the country could be necessary, and not only to
determine who polled a 40 percent plurality but also to determine if
anyone actually polled the 40 percent, and if not which two candidates
would be in the runoff. This means every vote for every candidate,
including the Left-Handed Vegetarians Party candidate, would have to

be reexamined under court supervision because it would be part of the total out of which at least one candidate would have to win 40 percent.

Change the rules and on election night it appears that we have a president-elect who, with 40.1 percent of the vote, has a margin of less than one percent over the runner-up. But wait, perhaps not. Fraud somewhere, or even a simple recording error that reverses the order of numbers could mean that no one polled the required plurality. Any of the candidates, not just the runner-up, could challenge because they all have potential to win something in a runoff in return for their endorsements. Weeks could go by without anyone knowing if we have a president-elect or if we have to go through a runoff election. And what will the candidates be doing while we're all waiting? Will they continue to campaign? Start negotiating with each other? This is far from a swift, sure, clean, and clear decision. It would be a national and even an international ordeal.

In a close, multi-candidate election this is likely. We have already had five elections in which the popular vote margin was less than one percent (in one case it was merely *one tenth of one percent*). But in all these cases the magnifier effect in the electoral vote system converted these slim margins into absolute electoral vote majorities for a swift, sure, clean, and clear decision. Should this benefit be sacrificed so that we have a more accurate reflection of the popular will? This is to sacrifice something for nothing. We already know what the popular vote percentages are in presidential elections. Even with the electoral vote system, the media told us that Clinton polled 43 percent of the popular vote, and lest we forget, the Republicans bring it up with some frequency since it made him a minority president. If he had polled 61 percent of the popular vote, the Democrats would have continually reminded us of that fact.

The advocates of direct nonfederal election make much of the fact that their system would prevent a runner-up president, and that the current system has produced one—Benjamin Harrison, who won an electoral vote majority though Cleveland beat him in the popular vote with a margin of *eight tenths of one percent* after running a sectional campaign. Is this really so awful? Why is it more democratic to have a 40 percent president than to have a 47.86 percent president who was a runner-up by a mere whisker? Cleveland didn't even win a majority of the popular votes. A logical majoritarian would have to say that there should have been a runoff election. Is the most votes—no matter how narrow the margin or how the votes are distributed in the country—a sacred principle instead of a rather arbitrary method of estimating the will of the people? Not all of the people vote, and voting doesn't reflect the intensity of preferences.

To illustrate my point, at the institution where I teach, a proposal to change the liberal arts graduation requirements for all students was put to a vote of all faculty and nonteaching professionals and ended in a tie. Suppose it had received one more vote. If you were president of the institution would you authorize it? Do you think the faculty would support rather than resist the plan simply because it had one more favorable than unfavorable vote? When the tie was announced, many faculty (and not just political scientists) asked for information on the distribution of the vote. They wanted to know how the arts and sciences faculty voted because they would be the ones who would teach the courses. Implicit in this question was the general opinion that if the arts and sciences faculty stood behind the program, authorizing the plan would be one thing, but if they stood against, it would be quite another. The distribution of a vote can be a very important factor especially in a tie or near tie. In this case the functional vote-distribution requirement was a deep arts and sciences base. In presidential elections the functional vote-distribution requirement is a broad federal base.

When I first heard the result of this faculty vote, I was worried that our president would "break the tie" and adopt the proposal anyway, but I needn't have. The president was not a mathematician, he was a political scientist, and so the proposal was rethought and renegotiated. With presidential elections we do not have time for academic niceties. We need a tie breaker. The Harrison/Cleveland contest verged on a draw. When you must have a swift decision and you have a draw you need some device to break the tie. The tie-breaking device of the electoral vote system amounts to whoever wins the most states. Harrison won a majority of the states. If anything, the Harrison/ Cleveland election serves as an object lesson to candidates warning them against a sectional strategy.

Since the electoral vote system magnifies the plurality winner's margin of victory unless his support is not properly (politically) distributed, a win-the-most-states tie breaker is quite reasonable in a continental nation. On a cost-benefit basis, in presidential selection, a system that requires broad, cross-national support is worth the risk of a runner-up president when the election is a near draw.

Unless one has an accountant's perspective on democracy, direct non-federal election is not more democratic. It won't tell us anything about the national popular vote that we don't already know. It claims that no runner-up will be victorious under its system, but because its victory requirement is not a majority but only a 40 percent plurality, its claim is a mere formality, devoid of any real meaning. Without a runoff in every case when no one wins a majority of the popular votes, we cannot know which of the top two candidates is the actual runner-up. As it has no real benefits, it has rather high costs. It delegitimizes the federal principle in all our institutions, works against a swift, sure, clean, and clear decision, undermines our moderate, coalition building and thus stabilizing two-party system, and because it has no vote-distribution requirement, can diminish the victor's capacity to govern.

Other Reform Proposals

Though their heyday has probably passed, there are two other reform proposals that have attracted congressional support, the district and proportional plans. They both would retain the electoral votes and prohibit the winner-take-all rule. Under the district plan the popular votes to determine two of the electoral votes (the "senatorial two") would be cast at large to reflect the statewide constituency, the remainder of a state's electoral votes would be determined by the popular votes cast in districts created by the state legislature. Under the proportional plan the popular votes would be cast and counted statewide but the electoral votes would be allotted on the basis of the proportion of popular votes. Thus if Clinton won 53 percent of the vote in New York he would win 53 percent of New York's electoral votes. Proportional plans also usually have a 40 percent plurality rather than a majority of the electoral votes victory requirement.

The district plan would bring the odious and seemingly insurmountable problem of gerrymandering in its wake. The proportional plan is so complex and unwieldy that it would gladden an accountant's heart. Popular vote percentages would have to be calculated to three decimal points, and this on a state by state basis. At least fifty electoral votes, one for each state, could go one way or another and to various candidates, depending on three decimal point percentages. And these three decimal points could determine not only who won, but whether anyone did. These three decimal points in fifty states could determine if a runoff was necessary and if so which candidates would be in the running. You want to talk about complex! Compared to this, the current electoral vote system is a snap. The problems of gerrymandering and of three decimal point calculations for numerous candidates in

fifty states should suffice to indicate why these plans are going no-
where. There is no need for extended analysis of either of these plans
since many of the criticisms of the direct nonfederal plan apply to
both, including especially far more frequent contingency elections and
the weakening of our moderate, coalition building two-party system.

There is another alternative proposal called the national bonus plan,
proposed by a task force of the Twentieth Century Fund. This plan
would abolish the office of elector and have the electoral votes allocated automatically on a winner-take-all basis to the winner of a
popular plurality in each state. It would also create a bonus pool of
two electoral votes for each state and the District of Columbia. This
bonus pool of 102 votes would be awarded on a winner-take-all basis
to the candidate with the most popular votes nationwide. To be elected
to the presidency a candidate would have to win a majority of electoral
votes (under its proposal 321 out of a total of 640). If no candidate
achieved a majority there would be a runoff between the two top
candidates within thirty days, and the candidate who won a majority
of electoral votes in the runoff would be the president.

The goals of this plan are to prevent a runner-up president, to
eliminate the possibility of faithless electors, to preserve the federal
principle in presidential elections, and to support the two-party system. These are all desirable goals, but there is question as to whether
the plan succeeds in accomplishing them. A bonus of 102 electoral
votes is a great prize and could of itself encourage multiple candidates
to enter. Furthermore, the very existence of a popular vote runoff
increases the incentive for voters to cast a protest vote or to vote for
third-party or independent candidates in the belief they would have a
second chance to vote. As a result there are fears that the proposal
could convert the general election into a national primary.

Further, if this plan encouraged multiple candidacies it could also
lead to a president who polled far less than 40 percent of the popular
vote. The bonus plan reduces the number of state electoral votes
needed to win from the current 270 to 219. (A majority of the current
538 electoral votes is 270, but under the bonus plan the total number
of electoral votes would be an inflated 640 of which a majority is 321,
including the 102 bonus votes, and so only 219 state electoral votes
plus the bonus votes would give victory.) This means that in a multiple-
candidate race, a candidate could win the office because he won the
electoral votes in the eight largest states as well as the bonus electoral
votes with pluralities in the range of 33 to 35 percent.

Additionally, there is concern about disputes over who actually won the national popular vote contest and thus the pool of 102 electoral votes. We have had a great many close elections in our history, and in a close election a candidate would have a great incentive (102 electoral votes) to demand a court-ordered recount of every voting precinct, leading to uncertainty and delay. It might be impossible to have a runoff within the thirty-day period.

Although some think tanks have endorsed this plan, it has not made much headway in Congress very probably because the bonus votes reduce the value of the electoral votes of the smallest states. The 102 bonus electoral votes are more than the combined electoral votes of the seventeen smallest states and the District of Columbia (five or less electoral votes each). In fact, the bonus votes are more than the combined electoral votes of twenty-two states and the District of Columbia (seven or less electoral votes each). This makes it unlikely that there would be enough states willing to support a constitutional amendment for the bonus plan. Since thirty-eight states must ratify an amendment, it takes only thirteen states to defeat one.

Most supporters of an all-national election aren't satisfied with this plan, and most supporters of a federal election are sufficiently satisfied with the current system or would be satisfied with minor changes such as abolishing the office of elector. And because the bonus plan inflates the electoral vote system, it is questionable whether it actually serves the federal principle and its requirement for a broad distribution of the popular vote. As a result there is no real momentum for the bonus plan. Even some of its supporters advocate proceeding with caution.

Why does the Electoral College keep on winning? It's not perfect, but it beats the alternatives. All things considered, it has a darn good track record. Those who would radically change it keep reminding us of Murphy's first law—"anything that can go wrong will go wrong." True enough, though that usually happens sooner rather than later, and we have had 160 years of reasonably successful experience under the current system. As William C. Kimberling has pointed out, "For the past hundred years, the Electoral College has functioned without incident in every presidential election through two world wars, a major economic depression and several periods of acute civil unrest. Such stability, rare in human history, should not be lightly dismissed."[1] It's one thing to tinker with your car engine, or to experiment with a soup recipe; it's quite another to tinker with the Constitution or experiment with the supports for the federal principle. When it comes to the Constitution most of us say: let well enough alone. We are a busy, practical people who instinctively understand that the demand for the perfect is the enemy of the good.

The radical reformers need to be informed of Murphy's unpublished second law, the law of unintended consequences—Reform has a twin called Deform. It is not enough to point out possible problems in a process that has borne the test of time. The burden of proof that their cure is not worse than the disease must be borne by the advocates of all reforms. The Electoral College keeps winning because they have not.

Notes

1. William C. Kimberling, *The Electoral College* (Washington, D.C.: National Clearinghouse on Election Administration, Federal Election Commission, 1992), 7.

Chapter 6

The Constitutional Solar System

A constitution is not simply the highest and most solemn law a people can make, it is an organic arrangement of interdependent balanced parts. It is like a solar system where the entire system is dependent upon each planet being in its place, each moving in its own orbit around the sun, and if you change a part, you change the whole. The fundamental principles of the American Constitution are like the sun in the solar system. They are the center around which everything else in the Constitution rotates.

That constitutional center is composed of two principles: the separation of powers and the federal system. The role of the former (the division of the national government into three departments: executive, legislative, and judicial) is more widely understood and appreciated than the latter. In fact, one of the leading college texts on American government begins its chapter on federalism by saying, "A splendid way to guarantee a small attendance at a gathering, it is sometimes joked, is to hold a fund-raiser for a defeated candidate or schedule a meeting to discuss the merits of federalism."[1] Yet federalism is just as central to our constitutional solar system as the separation of powers. Both these principles affect the arrangement of all our national offices, an arrangement of consensus building through checking and balancing. The electoral vote system in presidential elections not only is a part of this constitutional solar system, it is the paradigm, the very model of our democratic federal republic.

Nonetheless, there are some who think the federal principle is unfair and undemocratic in presidential elections and ought to be abandoned in favor of an all-national election. They assert that the electoral vote system and the winner-take-all rule create "wasted" and "lost" votes, thereby disfranchising people and restricting and diminishing their voting power.

The "wasted" vote is any vote in excess of the plurality a candidate needs to win all of a state's electoral votes. If you voted for Clinton in Wisconsin in 1992, and if he won the plurality there by two votes, one of them was "wasted" in the sense that your vote and any others in excess of a bare plurality would have been more useful to him if cast in Texas, which he lost. From Clinton's perspective, trying to win every vote or win by an enormous margin in Wisconsin would be a waste of his limited campaign resources. From his perspective it would be better to win lots of states than only a few by landslides. The possibility of "wasted votes" gives candidates the incentive to build broad cross-national majorities.

From the individual voter's perspective it looks quite different. How could you or anyone know whether the "wasted" vote in Wisconsin was yours rather than some other person's vote? And how could you or anyone else know until after the election precisely how many votes Clinton would need to gain the plurality in Wisconsin and thus whether your vote for him would be "wasted"? To call your vote wasted is like saying that your run in the fifth inning of the first game of the World Series was "wasted" because your team won the game by three runs. One could just as easily call such a vote an "insurance" vote or a "mandating" vote.

The "lost" vote is any popular vote that does not produce some electoral votes. If you vote for a candidate who loses in your state (in 1992, a vote for Clinton in Texas, for Bush in Minnesota, or any vote for Perot (since he did not win any states), according to these critics, you have "lost" your vote. But of course if you cast it, and if there was no fraud, which no election system can totally prevent, you didn't lose it. It was counted in your state for your candidate. Your candidate lost in your state, but you did not lose your vote.

The critics contend, however, that because you couldn't combine your vote with those of like-minded folk across state lines your vote, though cast, was ineffective. This is not so either. Your vote was counted as part of the total state and the total national popular vote, and thus it had political impact. It was part of Clinton's 43 percent, or Bush's 38 percent or Perot's 19 percent. As such it was a determining factor in the size and shape of the popular mandate. Your vote had political effects indicating not only the size but the distribution of opinion about the various candidates and about the direction of various policies. Pundits spent months analyzing the results of the election of which your vote was a part, and all politicians, including the president, pay attention to these analyses.

But your vote did not help give your candidate any electoral votes, so it was "lost" in that sense at least. Still, if your candidate won the presidency, what kind of loss is this? You're a winner. If your candidate lost in both the popular vote and electoral vote contests, he shouldn't be president. You lose and you ought to. In any kind of election those who vote for the losing candidate have "lost" their votes unless we divide the office. If we had done that in 1992, Clinton would have been president for 43 percent, Bush for 38 percent, and Perot for 19 percent of the four-year term. To sacrifice the unity and stability of the office in the name of formal voter equality is too frightful to contemplate. The bottom line is that every election for a single, unified office is, and for good reason must be, a winner-take-all contest.

It is the third possibility that clarifies the issue. Your candidate won the popular vote contest but lost in the electoral vote—win-states—contest. But that happens very rarely and only when a candidate fails to build broad cross-sectional support. Your team scored the most runs in the series, but the World Series is determined by winning four games out of seven not by most overall runs scored. The issue is the validity of the federal principle, the requirement that the victorious candidate must win states. Why is the baseball championship determined by a series of games rather than a single-game run-scoring contest? Baseball fans will answer that a series of games provides a better overall assessment of the strengths and weaknesses of the competing teams.

Why should the presidential contest be determined by the necessity to win states? Same reason: to provide a better overall assessment of the strengths and weaknesses of the competing candidates. To govern this continental, heterogeneous, federal republic, the president needs to have broad, cross-national support. The federal principle in presidential elections not only creates the incentive for candidates to build such support, it also is the test of which candidate has the best claim to such support. The federal principle is not an unfair limitation on voters. Like being thirty-five years of age, it is actually a politically reasonable qualification for the presidency.

And if the issue is really formal voter equality, why is it more important to have formal voter equality in electing the president than in electing a senator or congressman? In every districted election some people "lose" and others "waste" their votes. In every districted election people are prevented from combining their votes with those of like-minded partisans across district lines. In the Senate and House races the candidate who wins a plurality in the election wins 100 percent of the office. As a result the majority party in each chamber of Congress is invariably "overrepresented." If we aggregated the votes for representatives in Congress nationally, the majority party in Congress would have far less power than it does now. If a districted election is unfair in presidential elections, it is unfair in congressional elections and should be abolished there as well. Those who wonder why the direct nonfederal election plan has failed to pass the Senate and the House might consider that many members of Congress are quite conscious of the fact that this attack on the federal principle cannot be limited to the presidency.

The critics would have us abandon the federal principle in presidential elections and believe that if we make this change nothing else will change or change for the worse. But to change only the system of presidential elections could greatly increase the power and prestige of the presidency at the expense of Congress. On their own definition of what constitutes legitimacy, a president chosen by an all-national majority could claim to have a more authentic mandate from the people than the members of Congress still chosen under the federal principle. He could claim to be the only voice for the national interest. At its best Congress speaks for what John C. Calhoun called a concurrent majority—a majority built out of a temporary and changing coalition of state and local interests. The separation of powers was designed to create a balance of coequal policymaking branches; it was designed to make rivals of the president and Congress. Rivals are opponents of equal or nearly equal strength, either one of which may defeat the other on a given day. As the claimant of the support of the only all-national majority, the president's influence would be greatly inflated in a nation that has declared the federal principle to be undemocratic.

If the federal principle is a democratic heresy, we ought to abandon it for all of our institutions. If the federal principle is unfair in presidential elections, why shouldn't we abandon it for the Senate? If numbers of voters are the only test for legitimacy then the Senate is unfair. A state with half a million people has the same representation as a state with twenty million people, and this in the Senate, which alone passes on Supreme Court nominations and treaties. And then surely the amendment procedure is also unfair. Why should each state have an equal vote on constitutional amendments? To allow this means that a no vote by a state with half a million people cancels a yes vote by a state with twenty million people. Why don't we forget the states altogether and have an all-national, direct popular vote on constitutional amendments?

In fact, if all we are interested in is avoiding "lost" and "wasted" votes, then nothing short of direct majority-rule democracy—no representatives at all—will do it. You voted for Bush because of his "no new taxes" promise and for your senator because of his endorsement of that pledge. When they reneged, your vote was lost and wasted. If all that matters is giving people the opportunity for self-expression and for giving them equally weighted votes, then why don't we abolish Congress entirely and vote directly on all policy questions? Soon we should have the machinery to do this in an electric town meeting. What shall we do about the problem in the former Yugoslavia? Press A for economic sanctions. Press B for removing the arms embargo. Press C for send in the Marines. Press D for nuke them all. The founders would roll over in their graves. A head count is not a political process.

There are some who argue that the people should have a direct all-national vote for the president because he represents them all. If so why shouldn't we have a direct all-national vote on constitutional amendments, which rule and limit us all? And why shouldn't we have a direct all-national vote on Supreme Court Justices, who interpret *our* Constitution?

The founders knew the answer to all these questions. I can almost hear their voices crying: Beware of majority tyranny! The founders were partisans of popular government; they actually believed that the people can be trusted to govern themselves—if they are provided the proper political process. The founders concluded that the federal system was an essential part of the proper process because it preserves diversity while using that diversity to build national unity. It infuses diversity into the national government.

Alexis de Tocqueville, commenting on the federal principle, called it "a wholly novel theory, which may be considered as a *great discovery* in modern political science."[2] It was so novel that Tocqueville said the term "federal" is not adequate to describe it. The "great discovery" establishes compound binary citizenship. Americans must obey two governments; we are citizens of two unequal societies, one state and subordinate, the other national and supreme; each of these two governments rules us directly and enforces its own laws.

As a U.S. citizen and a citizen of New York, I must pay taxes to both, taxes levied separately and paid by me directly to the two different governments. If I fail to pay the national tax, agents of the national government will arrest me, and I will be tried in a national court. In a federal system, as the term was defined in Tocqueville's time, the general government would pass a tax that had to be paid by the state governments. In such a system I would pay a tax to New York, and New York would pay a tax to the general government. If I failed to pay the tax, agents of New York would arrest me, and I would be tried in a New York court. The general government could not arrest me or try me in its own court. I would be a citizen of New York, and New York per se would be a member of a permanent league of states. In a national system properly so called, I would pay a tax to the national government, which would use some of it to fund the local operations of its agents. I would be a citizen of the United States living in a region called New York, but I would not be a citizen of New York because New York would not be a state properly. It would not have a separately created government.

For want of a better term, Tocqueville called this novel system "an incomplete national government."[3] But that doesn't work either, for the word "incomplete" suggests a deficiency that belies his assertion that this new form of government is "a great discovery." Madison was more accurate, in *Federalist* 39, when he said that our form of government "is, in strictness, neither a national nor a federal Constitution, but a composition of both."

In this light we may begin to understand why what we call the federal principle is a great new invention. It is a compound, or rather an alloy. An alloy is a mixture formed by the fusion of two or more metals, as brass is a combination of copper and zinc. And why do we combine these two metals? Brass is harder and more ductile and malleable than copper. We create alloys because they combine the advantages of several different and separate things. Steel alloys can make things simultaneously stronger and lighter or tougher, or all three.

Tocqueville intuitively understood that what we have called the federal system has the properties of an alloy, for he says its advantage is to unite the benefits and thereby to avoid the weaknesses of small and large societies. It unites the strength, and wealth and capacity to pursue the great scientific, artistic, and other social enterprises of large societies with the liberty found in small ones. And by fusing the two it creates a flexibility and diversity otherwise not found in powerful large societies. The fusion occurs because the national government is built out of representatives selected on the federal principle of common state citizenship. The national government is supreme and national citizenship is primary, but the fusing process creates a new kind of nation, a new kind of citizenship—one that can recognize and preserve diversity within its powerful national unity.

Should we abandon this federal system for a purely national one or is the federal system worth preserving? Consider its many advantages. It is vital to individual liberty because it prevents the formation of all-national majority factions. And it contributes to individual liberty because, while the states are not supreme, they do have authority in some areas and pass different laws on state and local taxes, on marriage and divorce, on health and drug regulations, on business and labor, on crime, on educational systems, and on the environment. And they also administer many of the national laws and so can adapt them to local conditions. Because state laws differ and because state administration of national laws varies in order to be sensitive to local needs, people can vote with their feet. They can move to another state whose laws and administrative policies they prefer. The federal system protects the individual's freedom to make more of his own choices.

In addition, the states provide a margin for survival in case of attack. If Washington, D.C., is wiped out, gasified, there are still the fifty states to serve as alternative sources of authority, to provide government, and to rally the resistance. The states are also sources of experimentation and innovation. Many new policies (policies on education, welfare, crime or the environment) can be tried out simultaneously in various states. They can be tried out on a small scale as controlled experiments to see whether and how well they work before being adopted on the national level. The state governments are training grounds for national leaders; many of these leaders have served their internships in state and local governments before they were chosen to serve at the national level. They honed their skills in the minor leagues before they were moved up to the majors. And because the states exist it is easier to develop agreement on solutions to national problems. The national government does not have to decide every issue, set every policy because the states are there to take up the slack. Thus there is more time and energy to deal with truly national problems.

If the federal principle is unfair and undemocratic in presidential elections, it is unfair and undemocratic in all of our national elections. And it is unfair in the whole solar system of our Constitution. Attacks on the legitimacy of the federal principle cannot be confined; they will and must extend to the Senate (indeed to the Congress as a whole) and to the process of amending the Constitution.

Why does the Electoral College keep on winning? Because the electoral vote system is a model of our federal Constitution—a novel system, "a great discovery," that creates one society out of many societies. The reason is there for us to see on every nickel we spend. It is our national motto: E Pluribus Unum.

Notes

1. James MacGregor Burns et al., *Government by the People, National Version* (New Jersey: Prentice Hall, 1993), 51.

2. Alexis de Tocqueville, *Democracy in America*, Vol. 1 (New York: Random House, Vintage Books, 1945), 162.

3. *Democracy in America*, 164.

Appendix A

Alabama	9	Missouri	11
Alaska	3	Montana	3
Arizona	8	Nebraska	5
Arkansas	6	Nevada	4
California	54	New Hampshire	4
Colorado	8	New Jersey	15
Connecticut	8	New Mexico	5
Delaware	3	New York	33
Dist. of Columbia	3	North Carolina	14
Florida	25	North Dakota	3
Georgia	13	Ohio	21
Hawaii	4	Oklahoma	8
Idaho	4	Oregon	7
Illinois	22	Pennsylvania	23
Indiana	12	Rhode Island	4
Iowa	7	South Carolina	8
Kansas	6	South Dakota	3
Kentucky	8	Tennessee	11
Louisiana	9	Texas	32
Maine	4	Utah	5
Maryland	10	Vermont	3
Massachusetts	12	Virginia	13
Michigan	18	Washington	11
Minnesota	10	West Virginia	5
Mississippi	7	Wisconsin	11
		Wyoming	3

Total Electoral Vote 538
Needed to Elect 270

Appendix B

POPULAR AND ELECTORAL VOTES IN PRESIDENTIAL ELECTIONS, 1789–1992

Year	Major Candidates	Popular vote %	Electoral vote
1789	**George Washington**		69
	John Adams		34
1792	**George Washington**		132
	John Adams		77
1796	**John Adams**		71
	Thomas Jefferson		68
1800	**Thomas Jefferson**		73*
	Aaron Burr		73
1804	**Thomas Jefferson**		162
	Charles C. Pinckney		14
1808	**James Madison**		122
	Charles C. Pinckney		47
1812	**James Madison**		128
	DeWitt Clinton		89
1816	**James Monroe**		183
	Rufus King		34
1820	**James Monroe**		231
	John Quincy Adams		1
1824	**John Quincy Adams**	30.5	84**
	Andrew Jackson	43.1	99
	Henry Clay	13.2	37
	William Crawford	13.1	41
1828	**Andrew Jackson**	56.0	178
	John Quincy Adams	44.0	83

* Under the original plan the electors were to cast two votes for president, not one for president and one for vice president. In the election of 1800 the intention of the electors was that Thomas Jefferson would be president and Aaron Burr vice president. The tie in the electoral votes led to a contingency election in the House of Representatives. Because of this, the Constitution was amended to allow the electors to distinguish their votes for these offices. (See Twelfth Amendment.)

** The election of 1824 was decided by a contingency election in the House of Representatives. Although Andrew Jackson appears to have a higher percentage of the popular vote than the winner, John Quincy Adams, the popular vote cannot be determined: in six of the twenty-four states there was no popular vote and the legislatures cast the electoral votes.

Year	Major Candidates	Popular vote %	Electoral vote
1832	**Andrew Jackson**	55.0	219
	Henry Clay	42.4	49
1836	**Martin Van Buren**	50.9	170
	William H. Harrison	36.7	73
1840	**William H. Harrison**	53.1	234
	Martin Van Buren	46.9	60
1844	**James K. Polk**	49.6	170
	Henry Clay	48.1	105
1848	**Zachary Taylor**	47.4	163
	Lewis Cass	42.5	127
1852	**Franklin Pierce**	50.9	254
	Winfield Scott	44.1	42
1856	**James Buchanan**	45.4	174
	John C. Fremont	33.0	114
	Millard Fillmore	21.6	8
1860	**Abraham Lincoln**	39.79	180***
	Stephen A. Douglas	29.40	12
	John C. Breckinridge	18.20	72
	John Bell	12.61	79
1864	**Abraham Lincoln**	55.0	212
	George B. McClellan	45.0	21
1868	**Ulysses S. Grant**	52.7	214
	Horatio Seymour	47.3	80
1872	**Ulysses S. Grant**	55.6	286
	Horace Greeley	43.9	66
1876	**Rutherford B. Hayes**	48.0	185
	Samuel J. Tilden	51.0	184
1880	**James A. Garfield**	48.3	214
	Winfield S. Hancock	48.2	155

*** Lincoln's name did not appear on the ballot in ten states. Full percentages are given as Lincoln won the lowest popular vote percentage in the history of the presidency.

Year	Major Candidates	Popular vote %	Electoral vote
1884	**Grover Cleveland**	48.5	219
	James G. Blaine	48.2	182
1888	**Benjamin Harrison**	47.8	233
	Grover Cleveland	48.6	168
1892	**Grover Cleveland**	46.0	277
	Benjamin Harrison	43.0	145
1896	**William McKinley**	50.8	271
	William J. Bryan	46.7	176
1900	**William McKinley**	51.7	292
	William J. Bryan	45.5	155
1904	**Theodore Roosevelt**	56.4	336
	Alton B. Parker	37.6	140
1908	**William H. Taft**	51.6	321
	William J. Bryan	43.1	162
1912	**Woodrow Wilson**	41.8	435
	Theodore Roosevelt	27.4	88
	William H. Taft	23.2	8
1916	**Woodrow Wilson**	49.3	277
	Charles E. Hughes	46.1	254
1920	**Warren G. Harding**	61.0	404
	James M. Cox	34.6	127
1924	**Calvin Coolidge**	54.1	382
	John W. Davis	28.8	136
	Robert M. La Follette	16.6	13
1928	**Herbert C. Hoover**	58.2	444
	Alfred E. Smith	40.8	87
1932	**Franklin D. Roosevelt**	57.3	472
	Herbert C. Hoover	39.6	59
1936	**Franklin D. Roosevelt**	60.7	523
	Alfred M. Landon	36.4	8
1940	**Franklin D. Roosevelt**	54.7	449
	Wendell L. Wilkie	44.8	82

Year	Major Candidates	Popular vote %	Electoral vote
1944	**Franklin D. Roosevelt**	52.8	432
	Thomas E. Dewey	44.5	99
1948	**Harry S. Truman**	49.5	303
	Thomas E. Dewey	45.1	189
	J. Strom Thurmond	2.4	39
1952	**Dwight D. Eisenhower**	55.2	442
	Adlai E. Stevenson	44.5	89
1956	**Dwight D. Eisenhower**	57.4	457
	Adlai E. Stevenson	42.0	73
1960	**John F. Kennedy**	49.9	303
	Richard M. Nixon	49.6	219
1964	**Lyndon B. Johnson**	61.1	486
	Barry M. Goldwater	38.5	52
1968	**Richard M. Nixon**	43.4	301
	Hubert H. Humphrey	42.7	191
	George C. Wallace	13.5	46
1972	**Richard M. Nixon**	61.3	520
	George McGovern	37.3	17
1976	**Jimmy Carter**	50.1	297
	Gerald R. Ford	48.0	240
1980	**Ronald Reagan**	51.0	489
	Jimmy Carter	41.0	49
1984	**Ronald Reagan**	59.0	525
	Walter F. Mondale	41.0	13
1988	**George Bush**	53.0	426
	Michael Dukakis	46.0	111
1992	**Bill Clinton**	43.0	370
	George Bush	38.0	168
	H. Ross Perot	19.0	0

Select Bibliography

Abbott, David, and James Levine. *Wrong Winner: The Coming Debacle in the Electoral College*. New York: Praeger, 1991.

American Bar Association. *Electing the President: A Report of the Commission on Electoral Reform*. Chicago: American Bar Association, 1967.

Berns, Walter, ed. *After the People Vote*. Washington, D.C.: AEI Press, 1992.

Best, Judith. *The Case Against Direct Election of the President: A Defense of the Electoral College*. Ithaca, N.Y.: Cornell University Press, 1975.

Bickel, Alexander. *Reform and Continuity: The Electoral College, the Convention and the Party System*. New York: Harper and Row, 1968.

Diamond, Martin. *The Electoral College and the American Idea of Democracy*. Washington, D.C.: American Enterprise Institute, 1977.

Glennon, Michael. *When No Majority Rules*. Washington, D.C.: Congressional Quarterly, 1992.

Kimberling, William. *The Electoral College*. Washington, D.C.: National Clearinghouse, Federal Election Commission, 1992.

Longley, Lawrence, and Alan Braun. *The Politics of Electoral College Reform*. New Haven, Conn.: Yale University Press, 1972.

McCaughey, Elizabeth, ed. *Electing the President: Report of the Panel on Presidential Selection*. New York: Center for the Study of the Presidency, 1992.

Peirce, Neal, and Lawrence Longley. *The People's President: The Electoral College in American History and the Direct-Vote Alternative*. Rev. ed. New Haven, Conn.: Yale University Press, 1981.

Polsby, Nelson, and Aaron Wildavsky. *Presidential Elections*. 4th ed. New York: Scribner's, 1976.

Sayre, Wallace, and Judith Parris. *Voting for President: The Electoral College and the American Political System*. Washington, D.C.: The Brookings Institution, 1970.

Twentieth Century Fund. *Report of the Twentieth Century Fund Task Force on Reform of the Presidential Election Process*. New York: Holmes and Meier, 1978.

U. S. Senate. Committee on the Judiciary. Subcommittee on the Constitution. *The Electoral College and Direct Election of the President.* Hearings, 102nd Cong., 2nd sess., July 22, 1992. Washington, D.C.: Government Printing Office, 1993.

Zeidenstein, Harvey. *Direct Election of the President.* Lexington, Mass.: D.C. Heath, 1973.

Part Two

Readings

Editor's Introduction

Judith A. Best

On July 10, 1979, in a roll-call Senate vote, a proposal to replace the federally based Electoral College with a direct all-national election was defeated decisively. The vote was fifty-one in favor and forty-eight against the direct election amendment, far short of the two-thirds or sixty-seven votes needed to propose amendments. Not only was the opposition bipartisan, with twenty Democrats and twenty-eight Republicans against, it also covered the ideological spectrum, with liberals and conservatives voting together against the change.

This vote was the culmination of thirteen years of almost continuous effort to reform the method of presidential selection. The most recent and concerted movement began in early 1966 when the American Bar Association, responding to the urging of President Lyndon Johnson and some congressional leaders, created a Commission on Electoral College Reform. In January 1967, the Commission issued its report recommending a direct all-national election. The ABA report provided both the direction of and the impetus for the reform movement from at least 1970. The Senate Committee on the Judiciary, Subcommittee on Constitutional Amendments, began the debate with hearings in early February of 1966. Additional Senate hearings were held in 1968, 1969, 1970, 1973, 1977, and 1979. Although the House of Representatives had passed a direct-election proposal in 1969 by a vote of 339 to 70, the proposal did not reach the Senate floor until 1979.

During the thirteen-year debate the issue gradually ripened. Scholars attempted to calculate which groups were most advantaged under the College and under various reform proposals. The academic community divided, and each side produced its own roster of experts in support of its case. Arguments were sharpened and some people even switched sides. But this long debate did bear fruit. We have gained a better understanding of how the current system works. Areas of agreement have been identified—almost no one wants independent electors or likes the current contingency process in the House of Representatives. The fundamental disagreement has been clarified and defined as a difference in constitutional philosophy—a difference about the federal principle and the role of presidential selection in a federal system. Although the Electoral College has not worked as the framers anticipated, it has been adapted through the years—especially by the unit rule or winner-take-all practice—to fulfill the federal nature of the Constitution. The defeat of the direct election proposal in 1979 can be directly attributed to support for the federal nature of the nation and its government.

Despite the solid defeat of the direct election plan in 1979, the Electoral College remains and will remain a controversial issue. The philosophical issue may have been identified and clarified, but it has not been resolved. The advocates of direct all-national election are sincerely convinced that the Electoral College is undemocratic and severely flawed. As Lawrence Longley put it in his Senate testimony in July 1992, "it can create political and constitutional crises in determining who should be President." Thirteen years after the decisive Senate roll-call vote, the candidacy of H. Ross Perot provoked great alarm that the House contingency election would be triggered. So once again the Senate Committee on the Judiciary, Subcommittee on the Constitution, held hearings. The conversion of Bill Clinton's 43 percent of the popular vote into 69 percent of the electoral vote may have convinced some but not all that a House contingency election is not likely to be triggered. And candidates who are disadvantaged by a process that supports a two-party system, like Perot, will renew the call for abolishing the College. Further, as Professor Longley's testimony indicates, the contingency election is not the only possibility that can raise the alarm; a faithless elector or the selection of a runner-up president or even a near miss will revive the debate. Until the Electoral College is either changed or abolished, it will remain an enduring question in American politics.

1

Statement of Lawrence D. Longley before the U.S. Senate Committee on the Judiciary Subcommittee on the Constitution July 21–22, 1992

Mr. Chairman, my name is Lawrence D. Longley, and I am Professor of Government at Lawrence University in Appleton, Wisconsin. Since 1985, I have also served as Co-Chair of the Electoral Systems Research Committee of the International Political Science Association.

The Institution

The electoral college is a highly imperfect method of electing the President of the United States. At best, it distorts campaign strategy and poorly represents the popular will. At worst, it can create political and constitutional crisis in determining who should be President. The 1992 election illustrates vividly these distortions and imperfections and further contains the potential for crisis in the electoral college.

The Electoral College at Its Best

The electoral college means of presidential election is of great significance, even when it produces a clear decision. The electoral college is not a neutral and fair counting device for tallying popular votes cast for President in the form of electoral votes. Instead, it counts some votes as more important than others, according to the state in which they are cast. As a result, these distortions of popular preferences greatly influence candidate strategy: certain key states, their voters, parochial interests, political leaders, and unique local factors, are favored. The electoral college election of the President also discriminates among types of candidates. Independent or third party contenders with a regional following have great opportunities for electoral college significance, while independent or third party candidates with broad-based but nationally distributed support may find themselves excluded from winning any electoral college votes. Even without receiving electoral votes, however, such candidates can prove decisive in terms of swinging large blocs of electoral votes from one major party candidate to the other. Finally, the electoral college can reflect inaccurately the popular will because of the action of faithless electors—individual electors who vote differently in the electoral college from the expectations of those who elected them.

In short, the electoral college is neither neutral nor fair in its counting of the popular votes cast for the President of the United States.

1. The electoral college is a distorted counting device.

There are many reasons why the division of electoral votes will always differ from the division of popular votes. Among these are the apportionment of electoral votes among the states on the basis of census population figures that do not reflect population shifts except every ten years, the assignment of electoral votes to states on a population basis rather than a voter turnout basis, the "constant two" constitutional allocation of two electoral votes equally to each state regardless of size, and the winner-take-all system for determining each state's entire bloc of electoral votes on the basis of a plurality (not even a majority) of popular votes.

As a result of the census determination of electoral votes, states that are growing quickly during the 1990s will not have their new population growth reflected in their electoral vote total until the census in the year 2000, which will establish the electoral college apportionment for each state for the presidential elections of 2004 and 2008. In other words, population changes in any state which will have occurred since 1990 will not be reflected in the 1992 electoral college and will not be taken into account in the electoral college for up to fourteen years, in the year 2004.

The electoral college also does not reflect differing levels of voter turnout, either over time, or among states. The electoral votes each state commands is constant for either two or three presidential elections (1984 to 1988, or 1992 to 2000) despite increases in voter turnout in a state or, alternatively, continued low levels of voter participation. In a classic example, Mississippi and Kansas both had an identical 8 electoral votes in the presidential election of 1960, but Mississippi had an astonishing low voter turnout of 25.5 percent, while Kansas had a far greater voter turnout of 70.3 percent. As a result, in that election, Mississippi enjoyed one electoral vote per 37,271 actual voters, while Kansas had but one electoral vote per 116,003 voters. It is indeed a curious feature of the electoral college that low levels of voter participation are rewarded.

It is in the "constant two" and "winner-take-all" characteristics of the electoral college that one finds the most significant distortions of the electoral college. The extra two electoral votes, regardless of population, provides an advantage to the very smallest states by giving them at least three electoral votes while their population might otherwise entitle them to barely one. However, the importance of the winner-take-all feature overshadows all the other distortions: by carrying New York or California—even by just the smallest margin of popular votes—candidate will win *all* of that state's 33 or 54 electoral votes. As a consequence, the electoral college greatly magnifies the political significance of the large electoral vote state—even out of proportion to the millions of voters living there.

2. Candidate strategy is shaped and determined by these distortions.

Strategists for presidential candidates know full well the importance of these distortions of the electoral college. In the 1992 election, candidates Bush, Clinton, and Perot will spend inordinate time in the largest states of the country. A candidate's day, an extra expenditure of money, a special appeal—any of these might be pivotal in terms of winning an entire large bloc of electoral votes—in the case of California, 54, or 20 percent of the 270 electoral votes needed to win. Candidates and their strategists do not look at the election just in terms of popular votes, but rather in terms of popular votes which can tilt a state's entire bloc of electoral votes.

In the case of a three candidate race—as in 1992—the plurality win and winner-take-all features take on a special significance. A candidate—be it Bush, Clinton, or Perot—does not need 50% of California's vote to win its entire bloc of 54 electoral votes. Forty percent or even 35% might well do it. A close three-way division of popular votes in a large state even further magnifies the pivotal value of that state.

3. The importance of a particular state's parochial interests, political leaders, and unique local factors are magnified by the electoral college.

As has been previously argued, the distortions of the electoral college lead candidates to focus on large, swingable states in order to win their large blocs of electoral votes. The best way of appealing to these states is, of course, to concern oneself with the issues and interests special to that state. As a consequence, candidates Bush, Clinton, and Perot are likely, in 1992, to be exceedingly articulate about the problems of Pennsylvania's coal fields or California's defense industry or New York City's crime rates. A special premium is also placed on the role of key large state political leaders who might be significant in that state's outcome. Mayors Dinkins of New York, Bradley of Los Angeles, and Goode of Philadelphia, as well as Governors Cuomo of New York, Edgar of Illinois, and Wilson of California will be consulted—and courted—by the candidates, as will leaders of the California Hispanic and New York Jewish communities. Local factional feuds and diverse issues in the large pivotal states will play an unusually major role in presidential campaign politics.

In contrast, other states will be neglected. Smaller states, where a narrow plurality win could at most tilt only 3 or 4 electoral votes, will be relatively ignored. Additionally evident will be the lack of candidate time given to states of any size that are viewed as "already decided." No candidate has incentive, under the electoral college, to waste his campaign time or resources on a state or region already likely to go for him—or against him. In short, Delaware, a very small state, is unlikely to be contested vigorously by any candidate; likewise, the Rocky Mountain states may well be conceded to Perot (or alternatively to Bush) and, as a consequence, be "written off" by all the candidates.

In short, the electoral college focuses candidates' attention and resources on those large states seen as pivotal, and away from voters in other states that are too small or that are seen as predictable in outcome. The political interests of the large, swingable states are more than amply looked after; those of the other states are relatively neglected.

4. The electoral college differs in impact on different types of candidates.

Besides the distorting effect of the electoral college in terms of voters, the electoral college also discriminates among candidates. The two major party nominees start off on a relatively equal footing as far as the electoral college goes, assuming each enjoys comparable potential in the large swingable states. Independent or third party candidates, however, differ greatly in their potential in the electoral college.

Regionally based independent or third party candidates—such as George Wallace in 1968 or Strom Thurmond in 1948—may enjoy potential benefits from the electoral college. Because of their regional strength, they can hope to carry some states and, with them, those states' entire blocs of electoral votes. Their popular vote need not even be an absolute majority in a state; a simple plurality of votes will suffice. In 1968, for example, major party candidates Richard Nixon and Hubert Humphrey together split slightly over 61 percent of the popular vote in Arkansas, while George Wallace, a regional candidate who nevertheless won only 38 percent of that state's vote, received 100 percent of Arkansas' electoral votes. Dixiecrat candidate Strom Thurmond in 1948 benefited significantly from such splits. While winning 1.1 million votes over-all, only 2.4 percent of the national popular vote, he carried four southern states. He received, consequently, 39 electoral votes—7.3 percent of the national electoral vote total or an inflation of almost three times over his national popular vote strength. Regional candidates can be advantaged by the electoral college's winner-take-all feature; this advantage is in addition to and separate from whatever benefits might conceivably result from such a candidate being able to deadlock the electoral college. (This latter possibility will be discussed subsequently.)

Independent or third party candidates with broad-based but nationally distributed support are, on the other hand, sharply *disadvantaged* by the electoral college. Without plurality support somewhere, such a candidate will be shut out of any electoral votes. Such was the problem which plagued independent candidate John B. Anderson in 1980. Unless his support had been sufficiently unevenly distributed among the states to allow him to win in some states, his voter support—even had it run as high as 20 to 30%—was destined to result in total eradication in the electoral college. A significant factor leading to the sharp decline of Anderson's popular support in 1980 resulted precisely from this feature of the electoral college: since his popular vote support was unlikely to carry any state and its electoral votes, a vote for Anderson was widely seen as a wasted one. As a result of this and other factors, his support dwindled sharply over the six months of his independent presidential candidacy from a high of some 24% to a final vote tally of 6.6%. A similar decimation of a third party candidate's strength occurred in the 1948 election. Former Vice President Henry A. Wallace ran in that year's presidential contest as the candidate of the Progressive party. He received virtually the same popular vote as Dixiecrat candidate Thurmond in the same election—1.1 million votes or 2.4 percent. While regional candidate Thurmond saw his strength swell into 7.3% of the electoral votes, however, Wallace's vote was completely wiped out by the electoral college. In 1966, less successful independent candidate Eugene McCarthy suffered a similar fate. Although he received around 750,000 popular votes, his votes totally disappeared in terms of electoral votes.

The problem here is more than just unfairness to nationally-based independent or third party candidates when their popular votes resulted in no electoral votes. A major factor limiting the support of these very same contenders is the view that a popular vote for them is a "wasted vote": "He can't win—at least in this state. I want to cast a vote that counts—a vote for one of the major candidates." This problem could constitute an enormously difficult one for Ross Perot—or alternatively Bill Clinton or George Bush—in 1992. As the election campaign comes to its conclusion, millions of voters who are possibly inclined to vote for one of these candidates may decide not to do so because of the electoral college. Voters may reason: "My preferred candidate—Perot (or Clinton or Bush)—isn't likely to carry this particular state. One of the other candidates will. I had best vote for one of them (or against one of them by voting for the other). I want to have my vote mean something in deciding the election."

There is, however, another way that a "third place" contender with widely distributed national appeal like Perot (or Clinton or Bush) could be truly significant in the 1992 election, even should he not be in a position to win a large number of electoral votes. This is by his candidacy and his votes being decisive in tilting some of the large, closely competitive states, and with them tilting the outcome of the national election between the other two candidates. Such was the role minor independent candidate Eugene McCarthy nearly played in 1976. Although he received less than one percent nationally of the popular vote, he received more votes in four states (Iowa, Maine, Oklahoma, and Oregon, totaling 26 electoral votes) than the margins in these states by which Ford defeated Carter. In these four states, McCarthy's candidacy may have swung those winner-take-all blocs of electoral votes to Ford. Even more significantly, had McCarthy been on the New York ballot, it is likely that his votes would have been sufficiently drawn from Carter's strength in that one state to have tilted New

York's bloc of 41 electoral votes to Ford instead of Carter. If New York had gone to Ford, he would have then won the election by thus securing an electoral college majority—this despite Carter's indisputable national popular vote majority.

The prospects of Ross Perot being decisive in the outcome of—or even winning—the 1992 election are, of course, presently unknown. Polls as of mid-year are unclear and somewhat contradictory as to his enduring support and as to whether his support comes principally from Bush or Clinton; further they do not speak meaningfully as to the final outcome in specific states in a three-way race. Such initial polls early in the campaign season are very fragile and momentary indicators indeed, and certainly cannot predict the dynamics of popular vote shifts in the crucial final months of the campaign. Most importantly, they also do not indicate conclusively how Perot's support, at whatever level, will translate into possible electoral votes for him, or into shifts of electoral votes in individual states between the major party candidates Bush and Clinton. Nevertheless, it is absolutely clear that, because of the presence of three electorally viable candidates, the electoral college, as a vote tabulating mechanism, will be an important and profoundly inequitable institution that will play a significant role in the presidential election of 1992.

In short, the electoral college at best treats candidates unequally, and creates enormous potential difficulties for many independent or third party candidates, difficulties which Ross Perot may or may not be able to overcome in 1992. Whatever their level of success, however, independent or third party candidates may have great significance in electoral outcomes because of the powerful impact of relatively few popular votes on tightly contested large marginal states where the determination of a substantial bloc of electoral votes may ride on small and shifting pluralities.

5. Faithless electors may further distort the popular will.

A final problem of the electoral college "at its best"—in other words while still producing a clear decision—lies in the potential occurrence of faithless electors. In seven of the eleven most recent elections we have seen an individual deciding, after the November election, to vote for someone other than expected. In each of these instances, however, such elector defections have been both singular in occurrence and insignificant in outcome. They do constitute, however, a distortion of the popular will. When one of the state of Washington's nine Republican electors decides, as in 1976, not to vote for the state's popular vote winner, Jerry Ford, the voters of Washington have lost a portion of their franchise.

Individual elector defections for whatever reason—strongly held issues or personal whim—have been of minor significance in the past. Such faithless electors, however, would likely proliferate in the instance of an election producing a very close electoral vote count. In any case, the occurrence of faithless electors, even on an individual basis, is one more way by which the electoral college fails—even when definitive in its choice—to reflect faithfully and accurately the popular vote. The electoral college is not a neutral and fair means of electing the President. Neither, as we shall now see, is it a *sure* way of determining who shall be President.

The Electoral College at Its Worst

The electoral college does not inevitably result in a clear determination of the election outcome. Rather, the result of the popular vote, when transformed into the electoral votes which actually determine the President, may be uncertain and unresolved through December and even into January.

1. In a very close electoral vote count, ambitious electors could determine the outcome.

Individual electors have defected from voter expectations in the past for highly individual reasons. In the case of an electoral college majority resting on a margin of but a few votes, electors seeking personal publicity or attention to a pet cause could withhold—or just threaten to withhold—their electoral votes from the narrow electoral vote winner.

The 1992 popular vote may well produce a relatively close election, especially if candidate Perot—as it now appears likely—should win a significant number of electoral votes. A clear majority of electoral votes for Bush or Clinton—or even Perot—might still result, but if that electoral vote majority of 270 rested on a thin margin of but a few votes, such an electoral vote majority could be hostage to elector threats and reconsiderations. Uncertainty and suspense over whether there actually would be an electoral vote majority when the electors voted in December would make the five week period following the November election a period of political disquiet.

2. An election can produce a divided verdict, with one candidate receiving the most popular votes and the other candidate winning the election in electoral votes.

An electoral outcome with a divided verdict might well be conclusive in the sense that the candidate with the majority of electoral votes would become President with little question of outright popular upheaval. The electoral college would be seen at its worst, however, in the effect of such a "divided verdict" election on the legitimacy of a President. Should a person be elected—or re-elected—as President despite having run clearly second in popular preference votes, his would be a presidency weakened in its ability to govern and to lead the American people.

Such divided verdict elections have occurred two or three times in our nation's history, the most recent indisputable case being the election of 1888 when the 100,000 popular vote of Grover Cleveland was turned into a losing 42% of the electoral vote. It might be noted that the electoral vote winner in 1888, Benjamin Harrison, lost the subsequent election of 1892 to Grover Cleveland, this time in both popular votes *and* electoral votes.

A divided verdict election is, of course, entirely possible in 1992, especially if at least two of the candidates run close to each other in popular votes. Our most recent close Presidential election, that of 1976, contained a real possibility of an electoral vote reversal of the popular preference. If a total of 9,244 votes had been cast for Ford instead of Carter solely in the two states of Ohio and Hawaii, Ford would have won those two states, with them a national total of 270 electoral votes, and thus the presidential election—despite Carter's clear lead in popular votes. One hesitates to contemplate the consequences had a non-elected President such as Jerry Ford been inaugurated for four more years as president after having been rejected by a majority of the American voters in 1976, his only presidential election.

3. An election may be undecided on election night with deals and actions by the electors at the mid-December electoral college meetings deciding the outcome.

The most frequently expressed fear about the electoral college concerns the possibility of an electoral college deadlock—no candidate winning an electoral vote majority on the basis of the election night results. Most analysts assume that, in this case, an undecided election would go directly to the House of Representatives in January. In fact, it is entirely possible that an apparent electoral college deadlock, based on the November returns, would set off a sequence of possible deals and actions including the electors themselves.

The 41 days between the 1992 election day, November 3, and the day on which the electors will meet in their respective capitals in 1992, December 14, would be a period of speculation, conjecture, and crisis. Most electors will follow party lines, but some might deviate in order to vote for the popular vote winner, or to help a candidate who had almost achieved an electoral vote majority. Certainly, this period would be a period of intense uncertainty and unease, as unknown and obscure presidential electors decided the outcome of the 1992 presidential election.

Such an occurrence is entirely possible in any close election, especially should a third-party or independent candidate such as Ross Perot be able to win a number of electoral votes. In the last presidential election marked by a third party candidate winning electoral votes, that of 1968, third party candidate George Wallace carried 45 electoral votes. In that election, had a total of 53,000 popular votes been cast differently in the three states of New Jersey, Missouri, and New Hampshire, Nixon would have lost his electoral vote majority and instead had only 269 electoral votes—one short of the necessary majority. In the 1976 election, even without the presence of an independent or third party candidate able to win electoral votes, the possibility also existed of an electoral college deadlock. If 11,960 popular votes in the two states of Delaware and Ohio had shifted from Carter to Ford, Ford would have carried those two states and won their 28 electoral votes. The results of the 1976 election, then, would have been *an exact tie in electoral votes*: 269 to 269! The presidency would have been decided *not* on election night, but through deals or switches at the electoral college meetings in December, or the later uncertainties of the House of Representatives.

4. If the electoral college fails to produce a majority in December, the extraordinary procedure would be followed of election of the President by the House of Representatives in January.

Election of the President by the House of Representatives would be an exceedingly awkward undertaking. According to the Constitution, voting in the House would be by equally weighed states, with an absolute majority of 26 states needed for a decision. The House would choose from among the top *three* candidates in electoral votes—no other "compromise" candidate could be considered.

Congressmen could be in a great quandary as the House started to vote on January 6, 1993. Many Representatives would vote strictly along party lines, totally ignoring any strength shown by an independent or third party candidate such as Ross Perot. Other House members might feel it appropriate or even politically necessary to vote for the candidate (the opposing major party contender or even an independent candidate) who had carried their district. Some House members might even feel influenced by the national popular vote result or by who had received the most popular votes in their state. In other words, should an election be thrown into the House, congressmen would vote in different ways for a number of different reasons. A final outcome would be difficult to predict, despite whatever partisan divisions existed.

As of 1992, the House is controlled by the Democratic party, not only in terms of the total number of seats, but also in terms of state delegations. Thirty-one state delegations have a Democratic majority, 10 are Republican, 8 are evenly divided between the two parties, and one state delegation (Vermont) consists solely of Socialist Representative Bernard Sanders. This Democratic favorable position as of mid-1992, however, is likely to be eroded by the results of the November 1992 House elections: fifteen of the Democratic state delegations presently have Democratic majorities by only one seat; a loss of one Democratic Representative in these fifteen states would make it either a tied or a Republican majority state. If the Republican party should gain two dozen or more House seats in the 1992 election—a widely anticipated possibility—the newly elected House which takes office on January 4, 1993, will almost certainly have significantly fewer state delegations with clear Democratic majorities.

Beyond such calculations, however, lurks the fact that such partisan projections do not take into account the previously mentioned factors of congressional voting in accord with district results, voting in correspondence with state vote outcome, voting influenced by the national popular vote results, or voting even in terms of personal preferences. Vermont, for example, is one of the seven states (Alaska, Delaware, Montana, North Dakota, South Dakota, and Wyoming are the others) which have only one congressman. Each of these seven Republicans individually would be able to cast one of the 26 House state votes which could elect the President and these seven congressmen would outvote the 177 total House members from the six largest states—California, New York, Florida, Texas, Pennsylvania, and Illinois. Vermont's lone congressman, as previously noted, is Socialist Bernard Sanders—who at one point hinted that he might cast his state's vote in a House election of the President for independent Ross Perot. In order to forestall such a possibility, Representative Sanders recently has been courted by both House Republican and Democratic leaders; the *Washington Post* described him at mid-year 1992 as "The Lonely Guy No More." Under any scenario, House voting for President would at best be confused as members sort out pressures of party, constituency, political self-interest, and personal preference.

5. A final and definitive decision by the House in January is by no means certain.

The House would commence its deliberations and voting on January 6, 1993, only 14 days prior to the constitutionally mandated Inauguration Day of January 20. Such a House vote would be divided in 1993 between Bush, Clinton, and Perot. No matter how this vote splits, no matter how many state delegations are divided and consequently not able to vote, the constitutional requirement of 26 state votes will remain. The House of Representatives might well find it difficult—or even impossible—to decide on a President as Inauguration Day approaches. It is entirely possible that the result of the 1992 election may continue to be deadlocked in the House of Representatives past the immovable date of January 20.

If no President has been elected by the House of Representatives by noon on January 20, the Twentieth Amendment provides that the Vice-President-elect shall "act as President." (The Vice-President probably would have been elected by the U.S. Senate since the voting there is one vote per Senator, and, most importantly, is limited to the top *two* contenders. A difficulty might arise if the Democratic presidential-vice-presidential ticket had run *third* in electoral votes, thus requiring the presumably Democratically-controlled Senate to choose only between Republican Vice-President Dan Quayle and Ross Perot's running mate for election as Vice President-elect and potentially as acting President.) The result of such a presidential election, then, would not be the decisive determination of a President, but rather the designation of a Vice President who would act as President. He would fill that office for an uncertain tenure, subject to possible removal at any time by renewed House voting later in his term—especially following the midterm congressional elections when, undoubtedly, the partisan balance in the House would shift to the disadvantage of the acting President. His would be a most unhappy and weakened presidency, subordinate to Congress because of his administration's congressional creation and possible termination, limited by a nonexistent electoral mandate, and crippled by uncertainty as to how long his temporary presidency could continue.

The electoral college in the 1992 election may, unhappily, exhibit some or even many of these shortcomings. On the other hand, the American people may be lucky once more in this election year and not be faced by crisis in the electoral college. In any case, the electoral college will be a crucial determining factor in the 1992 election—and possibly even in subsequent elections—shaping and distorting the popular will.

At its best, the electoral college operates in an inherently distorted manner in transforming popular votes into electoral votes. In addition, it has enormous potential as a dangerous institution threatening the certainty of our elections and the legitimacy of our Presidents. These defects of the contemporary electoral college cannot be dealt with by patchwork reforms such as abolishing the office of presidential elector. This distorted and unwieldy counting device must be abolished, and the votes of the American people—wherever cast—must be counted directly and equally in determining who shall be President of the United States. It is all too likely that the 1992 presidential election will finally provide the American public with indisputable evidence of the failings of the electoral college as a means of electing the people's President.

2

Statement of Gouverneur Morris in the Federal Convention of 1787

Editor's Note

The mode of presidential selection was a very difficult problem for the members of the Federal Convention. They struggled with the issue for several months and did not make a final decision on the Electoral College until the last days of the Convention. There were two related major issues that informed their debate: the independence of the office and the re-eligibility of an incumbent. The questions were how to choose a president who would be independent of any faction or existing, ongoing body, especially the Congress; to set a term long enough to produce stability yet short enough to make the president responsible and allow for his re-election; to provide a way to remove him from office for violation of his trust; and to avoid the dangers of cabal and corruption in the selection process. During the weeks of debate many alternative methods for choosing the president were proposed: by the national legislature, by the state legislatures, by the state governors, by the people, by special electors chosen for the purpose. They rejected election by the people at least twice: nine states to one on July 17th, and nine states to two on August 24th. They would decide on a plan (most often selection by Congress) and a few days later change their minds. In late August the matter was referred to a special committee, The Committee of Eleven, which gave its report on September 4th. The proposal in this report was the plan finally adopted. Gouverneur Morris's explanation of the Committee recommendation is reported by James Madison in his Debates in the Federal Convention of 1787.

Tuesday Sepr. 4. 1787. In Convention

M^r. Govr. Morris said he would give the reasons of the Committee and his own. The 1st was the danger of intrigue & faction if the appointm^t. should be made by the Legislature. 2. The inconveniency of an ineligibility required by that mode in order to lessen its evils. 3. The difficulty of establishing a Court of Impeachments, other than the Senate which would not be so proper for the trial nor the other branch for the impeachment of the President, if appointed by the Legislature, 4. No body had appeared to be satisfied with an appointment by the Legislature. 5. Many were anxious even for an immediate choice by the people. 6. The indispensable necessity of making the Executive independent of the Legislature.—As the Electors would vote at the same time throughout the U.S. and at so great a distance from each other, the great evil of cabal was avoided. It would be impossible also to corrupt them. A conclusive reason for making the Senate instead of the Supreme Court the Judge of impeachments, was that the latter was to try the President after the trial of the impeachment.

3

The Federalist Papers

No. 39

Editor's Note

After making the case that the form of government under the Constitution is republican, Madison addresses the question of whether the form of the government is national or federal. He concludes that it is neither but "a composition of both." And he says the source of the executive is mixed—"derived from a very compound source."

. . . "But it was not sufficient," say the adversaries of the proposed Constitution, "for the convention to adhere to the republican form. They ought with equal care to have preserved the *federal* form, which regards the Union as a *Confederacy* of sovereign states; instead of which they have framed a *national* government, which regards the Union as a *consolidation* of the States." And it is asked by what authority this bold and radical innovation was undertaken? The handle which has been made of this objection requires that it should be examined with some precision . . .

. . . First.—In order to ascertain the real character of the government, it may be considered in relation to the foundation on which it is to be established; to the sources from which its ordinary powers are to be drawn; to the operation of those powers; to the extent of them; and to the authority by which future changes in the government are to be introduced.

On examining the first relation, it appears, on one hand, that the Constitution is to be founded on the assent and ratification of the people of America, given by deputies elected for the special purpose;

but, on the other, that this assent and ratification is to be given by the people, not as individuals composing one entire nation, but as composing the distinct and independent States to which they respectively belong. It is to be the assent and ratification of the several States, derived from the supreme authority in each State—the authority of the people themselves. The act, therefore, establishing the Constitution will not be a *national* but a *federal* act.

That it will be a federal and not a national act, as these terms are understood by the objectors—the act of the people, as forming so many independent States, not as forming one aggregate nation—is obvious from this single consideration: that it is to result neither from the decision of a *majority* of the people of the Union, nor from that of a *majority* of the States. It must result from the *unanimous* assent of the several States that are parties to it, differing no otherwise from their ordinary assent than in its being expressed, not by the legislative authority, but by the people themselves. Were the people regarded in this transaction as forming one nation, the will of the majority of the whole people of the United States would bind the minority, in the same manner as the majority in each State must bind the minority; and the will of the majority must be determined either by a comparison of the individual votes, or by considering the will of the majority of the States as evidence of the will of a majority of the people of the United States. Neither of these rules has been adopted. Each State, in ratifying the Constitution, is considered as a sovereign body independent of all others, and only to be bound by its own voluntary act. In this relation, then, the new Constitution will, if established, be a *federal* and not a *national* constitution.

The next relation is to the sources from which the ordinary powers of government are to be derived. The House of Representatives will derive its powers from the people of America; and the people will be represented in the same proportion and on the same principle as they are in the legislature of a particular State. So far the government is *national*, not *federal*. The Senate, on the other hand, will derive its powers from the States as political and coequal societies; and these will be represented on the principle of equality in the Senate, as they now are in the existing Congress. So far the government is *federal*, not *national*. The executive power will be derived from a very compound source. The immediate election of the President is to be made by the States in their political characters. The votes allotted to them are in a compound ratio, which considers them partly as distinct and coequal societies, partly as unequal members of the same society. The eventual election, again, is to be made by that branch of the legislature which consists of the national representatives; but in this particular act they are to be thrown into the form of individual delegations from so many distinct and coequal bodies politic. From this aspect of the government it appears to be of a mixed character, presenting at least as many *federal* as *national* features.

The difference between a federal and national government, as it relates to the *operation of the government*, is by the adversaries of the plan of the convention supposed to consist in this, that in the former the powers operate on the political bodies composing the Confederacy in their political capacities; in the latter, on the individual citizens composing the nation in their individual capacities. On trying the Constitution by this criterion, it falls under the *national* not the *federal* character; though perhaps not so completely as has been understood. In several cases, and particularly in the trial of controversies to which States may be parties, they must be viewed and proceeded against in their collective and political capacities only. But the operation of the government on the people in their individual capacities, in its ordinary and most essential proceedings, will in the sense of its opponents, on the whole, designate it, in this relation, a *national* government.

But if the government be national with regard to the *operation* of its powers, it changes its aspect again when we contemplate it in relation to the extent of its powers. The idea of a national government involves in it not only an authority over the individual citizens, but an indefinite supremacy over all persons and things, so far as they are objects of lawful government. Among a people consolidated into one nation, this supremacy is completely vested in the national legislature. Among communities united for particular purposes, it is vested partly in the general and partly in the municipal legislatures. In the former case, all local authorities are subordinate to the supreme; and may be controlled, directed, or abolished by it at pleasure. In the latter, the local or municipal authorities form distinct and independent portions of the supremacy, no more subject, within their respective spheres, to the general authority than the general authority is subject to them, within its own sphere. In this relation, then, the proposed government cannot be deemed a *national* one; since its jurisdiction extends to certain enumerated objects only, and leaves to the several States a residuary and inviolable sovereignty over all other objects. It is true that in controversies relating to the boundary between the two jurisdictions, the tribunal which is ultimately to decide is to be established under the general government. But this does not change the principle of the case.

The decision is to be impartially made, according to the rules of the Constitution; and all the usual and most effectual precautions are taken to secure this impartiality. Some such tribunal is clearly essential to prevent an appeal to the sword and a dissolution of the compact; and that it ought to be established under the general rather than under the local governments, or to speak more properly, that it could be safely established under the first alone, is a position not likely to be combated.

If we try the Constitution by its last relation to the authority by which amendments are to be made, we find it neither wholly *national* nor wholly *federal*. Were it wholly national, the supreme and ultimate authority would reside in the *majority* of the people of the Union; and this authority would be competent at all times, like that of a majority of every national society to alter or abolish its established government. Were it wholly federal, on the other hand, the concurrence of each State in the Union would be essential to every alteration that would be binding on all. The mode provided by the plan of the convention is not founded on either of these principles. In requiring more than a majority, and particularly in computing the proportion by *States*, not by *citizens*, it departs from the national and advances towards the *federal* character; in rendering the concurrence of less than the whole number of States sufficient, it loses again the *federal* and partakes of the *national* character.

The proposed Constitution, therefore, even when tested by the rules laid down by its antagonists, is, in strictness, neither a national nor a federal Constitution, but a composition of both. In its foundation it is federal, not national; in the sources from which the ordinary powers of the government are drawn, it is partly federal and partly national; in the operation of these powers, it is national, not federal; in the extent of them, again, it is federal, not national; and, finally in the authoritative mode of introducing amendments, it is neither wholly federal nor wholly national.

PUBLIUS

No. 51

Editor's Note

Madison continues his discussion of the separation of powers. After explaining the necessity of "giving to those who administer each department the necessary constitutional means and personal motives to resist encroachments of the others," and stating the policy of "opposite and rival interests," Madison relates this policy directly to the federal principle. He calls the federal system a "double security . . . to the rights of the people," but judges it especially necessary to the rights of the minority.

. . . There are, moreover, two considerations particularly applicable to the federal system of America, which place that system in a very interesting point of view.

First. In a single republic, all the power surrendered by the people is submitted to the administration of a single government; and the usurpations are guarded against by a division of the government into distinct and separate departments. In the compound republic of America, the power surrendered by the people is first divided between two distinct governments, and then the portion allotted to each subdivided among distinct and separate departments. Hence a double security arises to the rights of the people. The different governments will control each other, at the same time that each will be controlled by itself.

Second. It is of great importance in a republic not only to guard the society against the oppression of its rulers, but to guard one part of the society against the injustice of the other part. Different interests necessarily exist in different classes of citizens. If a majority be united by a common interest, the rights of the minority will be insecure. There are but two methods of providing against this evil: the one by creating a will in the community independent of the majority—that is, of the society itself; the other, by comprehending in the society so many separate descriptions of citizens as will render an unjust combination of a majority of the whole very improbable, if not impracticable. The first method prevails in all governments possessing an hereditary or self-appointed authority. This, at best, is but a precarious security; because a power independent of the society may as well espouse the unjust views of the major as the rightful interests of the minor party, and may possibly be turned against both parties. The second method will be exemplified in the federal republic of the United States. Whilst all authority in it will be derived from and dependent on the society, the society itself will be broken into so many parts, interests and classes of citizens, that the rights of individuals, or of the minority, will be in little danger from interested combinations of the majority. In a free government the security for civil rights must be the same as that for religious rights. It consists in the one case in the multiplicity of interests, and in the other in the multiplicity of sects. The degree of security in both cases will depend on the number of interests and sects; and this may be presumed to depend on the extent of country and number of people comprehended under the same government. This view of the subject must particularly recommend a proper federal system to all the sincere and considerate friends of republican government, since it shows that in exact proportion as the territory of the Union may be formed into more circumscribed Confederacies, or States, oppressive combinations of a majority will be facilitated; the best security, under the republican forms, for the rights of every class of citizen, will be diminished; and consequently the stability and independence of some member of the government, the only other security, must be proportionally increased. Justice is the end of government. It is the end of civil society. It ever has been and ever will be pursued until it be obtained, or until liberty be lost in the pursuit. In a society under the forms of which the stronger faction can readily unite and oppress the weaker, anarchy may as truly be said to reign as in a state of nature, where the weaker individual is not secured against the violence of the stronger; and as, in the latter state, even the stronger individuals are prompted, by the uncertainty of their condition, to submit to a government which may protect the weak as well as themselves; so, in the former state, will the more powerful factions or parties be gradually induced, by a like motive, to wish for a government which will protect all parties, the weaker as well as the more powerful. It can be little doubted that if the State of Rhode Island was separated from the Confederacy and left to itself, the insecurity of rights under the popular form of government within such narrow limits would be displayed by such reiterated oppressions of factious majorities that some power altogether independent of the people would soon be called for by the voice of the very factions whose misrule had proved the necessity of it. In the extended republic of the United States, and among the great variety of interests, parties, and sects which it embraces, a coalition of a majority of the whole society could seldom take place on any other principles than those of justice and the general good; whilst there being thus less danger to a minor from the will of a major party, there must be less pretext, also, to provide for the security of the former, by intruding into the government a will not dependent on the latter, or, in other words, a will independent of the society itself. It is no less certain than it is important, notwithstanding the contrary opinions which have been entertained, that the larger the society, provided it lie within a practicable sphere, the more duly capable it will be of self-government. And happily for the *republican cause*, the practicable sphere may be carried to a very great extent by a judicious modification and mixture of the *federal principle*.

PUBLIUS

No. 68

Editor's Note

Hamilton's complacency about the presidential selection process may be astonishing to a modern reader, but it could not have lasted long, since the first problem with the original plan arose in the election of 1800 and led to the adoption of the Twelfth Amendment. He does, however, give an accurate account of the reasons why the members of the Convention adopted the Electoral College.

The mode of appointment of the Chief Magistrate of the United States is almost the only part of the system, of any consequence, which has escaped without severe censure or which has received the slightest mark of approbation from its opponents. The most plausible of these, who has appeared in print, has even deigned to admit that the election of the President is pretty well guarded. I venture somewhat further, and hesitate not to affirm that if the manner of it be not perfect, it is at least excellent. It unites in an eminent degree all the advantages the union of which was to be desired.

It was desirable that the sense of the people should operate in the choice of the person to whom so important a trust was to be confided. This end will be answered by committing the right of making it, not to any pre-established body, but to men chosen by the people for the special purpose, and at the particular conjuncture.

It was equally desirable that the immediate election should be made by men most capable of analyzing the qualities adapted to the station and acting under circumstances favorable to deliberation, and to a judicious combination of all the reasons and inducements which were proper to govern their choice. A small number of persons, selected by their fellow-citizens from the general mass, will be most likely to possess the information and discernment requisite to so complicated an investigation.

It was also peculiarly desirable to afford as little opportunity as possible to tumult and disorder. This evil was not least to be dreaded in the election of a magistrate who was to have so important an agency in the administration of the government as the President of the United States. But the precautions which have been so happily concerted in the system under consideration promise an effectual security against this mischief. The choice of *several* to form an intermediate body of electors will be much less apt to convulse the community with any extraordinary or violent movements than the choice of *one* who was himself to be the final object of the public wishes. And as the electors, chosen in each State, are to assemble and vote in the State in which they are chosen, this detached and divided situation will expose them much less to heats and ferments, which might be communicated from them to the people, than if they were all to be convened at one time, in one place.

Nothing was more to be desired than that every practicable obstacle should be opposed to cabal, intrigue, and corruption. These most deadly adversaries of republican government might naturally have been expected to make their approaches from more than one quarter, but chiefly from the desire in foreign powers to gain an improper ascendant in our councils. How should they better gratify this than by raising a creature of their own to the chief magistracy of the Union? But the convention have guarded against all danger of this sort with the most provident and judicious attention. They have not made the appointment of the President to depend on any pre-existing bodies of men who might be tampered with beforehand to prostitute their votes; but they have referred it in the first instance to an immediate act of the people of America, to be exerted in the choice of persons for the temporary and sole purpose of making the appointment. And they have excluded from eligibility to this trust all those who from situation might be suspected of too great devotion to the President in office. No senator, representative, or other person holding a place of trust or profit under the United States can be of the number of the electors. Thus without corrupting the body of the people, the immediate agents in the election will at least enter upon the task free from any sinister bias. Their transient existence and their detached situation, already taken notice of, afford a satisfactory prospect of their continuing so, to the conclusion of it. The business of corruption, when it is to embrace so considerable a number of men, requires time as well as means. Nor would it be found easy suddenly to embark them, dispersed as they would be over thirteen States, in any combinations founded upon motives which, though they could not be properly be denominated corrupt, might yet be of a nature to mislead them from their duty.

Another and no less important desideratum was that the executive should be independent for his continuance in office on all but the people themselves. He might otherwise to tempted to sacrifice his duty to his complaisance for those whose favor was necessary to the duration of his official consequence. This advantage will also be secured, by making his re-election to depend on a special body of representatives, deputed by the society for the single purpose of making the important choice.

All these advantages will be happily combined in the plan devised by the convention; which is, that the people of each State shall choose a number of persons as electors, equal to the number of senators and representatives of such State in the national government who shall assemble within the State, and vote for some fit person as President. Their votes, thus given, are to be transmitted to the seat of the national government, and the person who may happen to have a majority of the whole number of votes will be the President. But as a majority of the votes might not always happen to center on one man, and as it might be unsafe to permit less than a majority to be conclusive, it is provided that, in such a contingency, the House of Representatives shall elect out of the candidates who shall have the five highest number of votes the man who in their opinion may be best qualified for the office.

This process of election affords a moral certainty that the office of President will seldom fall to the lot of any man who is not in an eminent degree endowed with the requisite qualifications. Talents for low intrigue, and the little arts of popularity, may alone suffice to elevate a man to the first honors in a single State; but it will require other talents, and a different kind of merit, to establish him in the esteem and confidence of the whole Union, or of so considerable a portion of it as would be necessary to make him a successful candidate for the distinguished office of President of the United States. It will not be too strong to say that there will be a constant probability of seeing the station filled by characters pre-eminent for ability and virtue. And this will be thought no inconsiderable recommendation of the Constitution by those who are able to estimate the share which the executive in every government must necessarily have in its good or ill administration. . . .

PUBLIUS

4

The U.S. Constitution

Article II

Section 1 The executive Power shall be vested in a President of the United States of America. He shall hold his Office during the Term of four Years and, together with the Vice President, chosen for the same Term, be elected as follows.

Each State shall appoint, in such Manner as the Legislature thereof may direct, a Number of Electors, equal to the whole Number of Senators and Representatives to which the State may be entitled in the Congress: but no Senator or Representative, or Person holding an Office of Trust or Profit under the United States, shall be appointed an Elector.

The Electors shall meet in their respective States, and vote by Ballot for two Persons, of whom one at least shall not be an Inhabitant of the same State with themselves. And they shall make a List of all the Persons voted for, and of the Number of Votes for each; which List they shall sign and certify, and transmit sealed to the Seat of the Government of the United States, directed to the President of the Senate. The President of the Senate shall, in the Presence of the Senate and the House of Representatives, open all the Certificates, and the Votes shall then be counted. The Person having the greatest Number of Votes shall be the President, if such Number be a Majority of the whole Number of Electors appointed; and if there be more than one who have such Majority and have an equal Number of Votes, then the House of Representatives shall immediately chuse by Ballot one of them for President; and if no person have a Majority, then from the five highest on the List the said House shall in like Manner chuse the President. But in chusing the President, the Votes shall be taken by

States, the Representation from each State having one Vote; A quorum for this Purpose shall consist of a Member or Members from two thirds of the States, and a Majority of all the States shall be necessary to a Choice. In every Case, after the Choice of the President, the person having the greatest Number of Votes of the Electors shall be the Vice President. But if there should remain two or more who have equal Vote, the Senate shall chuse from them by Ballot the Vice President.

The Congress may determine the Time of chusing the Electors, and the Day on which they shall give their Votes; which Day shall be the same throughout the United States. . . .

Amendment 12

The Electors shall meet in their respective states, and vote by ballot for President and Vice-President, one of whom, at least, shall not be an inhabitant of the same state with themselves; they shall name in their ballots the person voted for as President, and in distinct ballots the person voted for as Vice-President, and they shall make distinct lists of all persons voted for as President, and of all persons voted for as Vice-President, and of the number of votes for each, which lists they shall sign and certify, and transmit sealed to the seat of the government of the United States, directed to the President of the Senate;—The President of the Senate shall, in presence of the Senate and House of Representatives, open all the certificates and the votes shall then be counted;—The person having the greatest number of votes for President, shall be the President, if such number be a majority of the whole number of Electors appointed; and if no person have such majority, then from the persons having the highest numbers not exceeding three on the list of those voted for as President, the House of Representatives shall choose immediately, by ballot, the President. But in choosing the President, the votes shall be taken by states, the representation from each state having one vote; a quorum for this purpose shall consist of a member or members from two-thirds of the states, and a majority of all states shall be necessary to a choice. And if the House of Representatives shall not choose a President whenever the right of choice shall devolve upon them, *before the fourth day of March next following*, then the Vice-President shall act as President, as in the case of the death or other constitutional disability of the President.* The person having the greatest number of votes as Vice-President, shall be the Vice-President, if such a number be a majority of the whole numbers of Electors appointed, and if no person have a majority, then from the two highest numbers on the list, the Senate shall choose the Vice-President; a quorum for the purpose shall consist of two-thirds of the whole number of Senators, and a majority of the whole number shall be necessary to a choice. But no person constitutionally ineligible to the office of President shall be eligible to that of Vice-President of the United States.

*Changed by the 20th Amendment—Ed.

Amendment 20

Section 1   The terms of the President and Vice President shall end at noon on the 20th day of January, and the terms of the Senators and Representatives at noon on the 3rd day of January, of the years in which such terms would have ended if this article had not been ratified; and the terms of their successors shall then begin. . . .

Section 3   If, at the time fixed for the beginning of the term of the President, the President elect shall have died, the Vice President elect shall become President. If a President shall not have been chosen before the time fixed for the beginning of his term, or if the President elect shall have failed to qualify, then the Vice President elect shall act as President until a President shall have qualified; and the Congress may by law provide for the case wherein neither a President elect nor a Vice President elect shall have qualified, declaring who shall then act as President, or the manner in which one who is to act shall be selected, and such person shall act accordingly until a President or Vice President shall have qualified.

Section 4   The Congress may by law provide for the case of the death of any of the persons from whom the House of Representatives may choose a President whenever the right of choice shall have developed upon them, and for the case of the death of any of the persons from whom the Senate may choose a Vice President whenever the right of choice shall have devolved upon them. . . .

5

Direct Popular Election of the President and Vice President of the United States

December 6, 1977.—Ordered to be printed

Mr. Robert C. Byrd (for Mr. Bayh), from the Committee on the Judiciary, submitted the following

REPORT
Together with Minority and Additional Views
[To accompany S.J. Res. 1]

The Committee on the Judiciary, to which was referred the resolution (S.J. Res. 1) proposing an amendment to the Constitution of the United States relating to the direct popular election of the President and the Vice President of the United States, having considered the same, reports favorably thereon, without an amendment and recommends that the joint resolution do pass.

The text of Senate Joint Resolution 1 is as follows:

Joint Resolution

Proposing an amendment to the Constitution to provide for the direct popular election of the President and Vice President of the United States.

Resolved by the Senate and House of Representatives of the United States of America in Congress assembled (two-thirds of each House concurring therein), That the following article is proposed as an amendment to the Constitution of the United States, which shall be valid to all

115

intents and purposes as part of the Constitution when ratified by the legislatures of three-fourths of the several States within seven years from the date of its submission by the Congress:

"SECTION 1. The people of the several States and the District constituting the seat of government of the United States shall elect the President and Vice President. Each elector shall cast a single vote for two persons who shall have consented to the joining of their names as candidates for the offices of President and Vice President. No candidate shall consent to the joinder of his name with that of more than one other person.

"SEC. 2. The electors of President and Vice President in each State shall have the qualifications requisite for electors of the most numerous branch of the State legislature, except that for electors of President and Vice President the legislature of any State may prescribe less restrictive residence qualifications and for electors of President and Vice President the Congress may establish uniform residence qualifications.

"SEC. 3. The persons joined as candidates for President and Vice President having the greatest number of votes shall be elected President and Vice President, if such number be at least 40 per centum of the whole number of votes cast.

"If, after any such election, none of the persons joined as candidates for President and Vice President is elected pursuant to the preceding paragraph, a runoff election shall be held in which the choice of President and Vice President shall be made from the two pairs of persons joined as candidates for President and Vice President who received the highest numbers of votes cast in the election. The pair of persons joined as candidates for President and Vice President receiving the greatest number of votes in such runoff election shall be elected President and Vice President.

"SEC. 4. The times, places, and manner of holding such elections and entitlement to inclusion on the ballot shall be prescribed in each State by the legislature thereof; but the Congress may at any time by law make or alter such regulations. The days for such elections shall be determined by Congress and shall be uniform throughout the United States. The Congress shall prescribe by law the times, places, and manner in which the results of such elections shall be ascertained and cleared. No such election, other than a runoff election, shall be held later than the first Tuesday after the first Monday in November, and the results thereof shall be declared no later than the thirtieth day after the date on which the election occurs.

"SEC. 5. The Congress may by law provide for the case of the death, inability, or withdrawal of any candidate for President or Vice President before a President and Vice President have been elected, and for the case of the death of both the President-elect and Vice-President-elect.

"SEC. 6. Sections 1 through 4 of this article shall take effect one year after the ratification of this article.

"SEC. 7. The Congress shall have power to enforce this article by appropriate legislation."

Senate Joint Resolution 1 proposes an amendment to the Constitution of the United States to abolish the antiquated electoral college and undemocratic "unit vote" system and substitute direct popular election of the President and Vice President. The proposed amendment provides, further, that in the unlikely event no candidate receives 40 percent of the popular vote, the President and Vice President will be elected in a runoff election between the two pairs of candidates receiving the highest number of votes. . . .

The Opponents' Arguments and Some Counterpoints

In the 10 years the proposal for the direct popular election of the President has been before the Congress, through many weeks of hearings and many days of floor debate, the arguments on this question have been sharpened and refined. The questions raised by the proposed amendments have been reviewed and commented upon by an extremely broad range of individuals and institutions in our society over a long span of years. Each of the arguments suggested by those who have voiced opposition to direct popular election has been carefully examined. A majority of the committee has found the arguments unconvincing.

The Effect of Direct Election on the Two-Party System

Opponents of direct election have alleged that abolition of the electoral college would tend to proliferate the party structure and weaken the two major parties. They believe that the winner-take-all or unit rule feature of the present system is the most important institutional guarantee for the two-party system. A well known political scientist has summarized their argument as follows: "Under the present system, the votes cast for a minor party candidate in any state are lost except in the unlikely event he runs ahead of the major party candidate. On the other hand all of the votes cast for a minor party under a popular vote would count toward the total vote of its candidate. Therefore, the carryover of votes from state to state, which would be possible under direct election, would cause the proliferation of third parties".

However, a careful study of the dynamics of the electoral college reveals that it does not discourage third parties, and in certain instances actually encourages them. The strength of the two-party system and the deterrence of other types of nationwide third parties are related to factors other than the electoral college—factors which will not be affected by the adoption of direct election.

While opponents of direct election believe that the unit rule of the electoral college system discourages third parties, it is this very feature of the electoral college which has encouraged minor party candidates with the real possibility that they will be able to control or heavily influence an election. The electoral college engenders third parties in two respects. First, it provides incentives for the regional third party candidate such as George Wallace in 1968. Wallace perceived that by carrying a large bloc of States with a thin margin, he might be able to throw the two major candidates into a deadlock and thereby see the contest settled in the House of Representatives.

The winner-take-all rule also enhances the chances of national third-party candidates when they can gather votes in large, closely balanced states. For example, as Lawrence Longley testified before the subcommittee, Eugene McCarthy in 1976,

> with less than 1 percent of the popular vote, came close to tilting the election through his strength in close pivotal States. In four States, (Iowa, Maine, Alabama and Oregon) totaling 26 electoral votes, McCarthy's vote exceeded the margin by which Ford defeated Carter. In those States, McCarthy's candidacy may have swung those States to Carter. Even more significantly, had McCarthy been on the New York ballot, it is likely Ford would have carried that State with its 41 electoral votes, and with it the election—despite Carter's national vote majority.

Most authorities agree that the deterrence of third parties is related to factors other than the electoral college. An excellent case in point is the abortive attempt of the "peace" forces to organize a fourth party after the 1968 Democratic Convention. In 1968, "Peace Party" probably could not have garnered a plurality in enough states to have a significant impact on the electoral college, and the unit rule undoubtedly played some role in their ultimate decision not to proceed. However, it is difficult to believe that the organizers of the Peace Party in 1968 were any more deterred by the unit rule than were the organizers of the most successful nationwide third party in our history—the Republican party.

It is much more likely that the Peace Party failed in 1968 for two reasons totally unrelated to the structure of the electoral college—two reasons why nationwide third parties will also be deterred under direct election. First, as Richard Goodwin—one of those who attempted to organize the peace party—himself admitted, the organizers realized that their efforts would take votes from the major party candidate closest to them in conviction and insure the victory of the major party candidate most undesirable to them. The Peace Party would have been more apt to garner a Humphrey vote than a Nixon vote, and thus by entering the field they would have enhanced the prospects of Nixon. Second, nationwide third party movements are discouraged by the fact that they must compete with the major parties for a single office—the Presidency. Planners of a Peace Party in 1968 were discouraged by the realization that they would have little to show for their efforts, for unlike the European coalition governments, the Presidency is held by one person and would be the exclusive prize of one of the major parties. On the other hand, if all the Peace Party wanted was to "spoil" the Democratic Party's chances, then the electoral college system was best suited to its purposes. All they needed to do was to run in New York and California to insure a Democratic defeat.

Scholars who have studied the two-party system in this country and compared it to similar systems throughout the world have a variety of theories as to its cause; but none suggest the electoral college. Most political scientists believe that the major institutional influence on the two-party system is the election of almost all officials in the U.S. in single-member districts. This theory stems originally from the writings of Maurice Duverger, who has found that almost every government in the world which elects its officials from single-member districts and by plurality vote has only two major parties, while countries that use multi-member districts and proportional representation have a multitude of parties. Duverger and other scholars have found that the electoral mechanics of the single member district, in terms of its effect on the party system, are such that they tend to force factions to combine in order to be certain of capturing a popular vote plurality and victory.

It was the conclusion of the committee's majority that direct popular election would work affirmatively to strengthen the two-party system. First, by counting every popular vote regardless of where it is cast, direct election would spread and foster two-party competition on a nationwide scale. The goal of both major parties would be to "get out the vote" in every State. Simply carrying a State, the objective under the present system, would no longer be the ultimate objective. The critical point under direct popular election, in healthy contrast, would be the margin of victory—or, to view it from the opposite position, the margin of defeat. As a consequence, the likely winner would seek to maximize the State's net plus and the probable loser would work to minimize the State margin of defeat. The next result, therefore, would be increased party activity—particularly in what are now one-party States.

These arguments were given credence by the testimony of Douglas Bailey, media manager of the Ford-Dole 1976 campaign. It was Mr. Bailey's strong belief based on his personal experience in President Ford's general election campaign that, first, direct election would mean increased voting—now deterred by the electoral college system; second, direct election would mean a reduction—both of the dominance of and reliance on—impersonal media campaign communications and would significantly enhance participatory democracy. Finally, Mr. Bailey has come to the belief that "direct election would mean a strengthening of the two-party system and the local apparatus of both political parties."

Mr. Bailey brought up the fact that under the spending limits of public financing, local party organizations receive little help or attention from Presidential campaigns in the current electoral system—especially in states which are considered "sure" winners or "sure" losers. It was Mr. Bailey's opinion that because turnout becomes crucial with direct election and turnout is more a function of personal contact than media, local party organizations will receive greater campaign attention and resources as the most obvious existing vehicle for local contact, canvassing and turnout efforts. In his words,

> Under the current system of spending limits, new spending for new needs will mean less spending for old needs. . . . Thus, direct election not only would mean that every vote and every voter counted but it would help involve the people in the campaign process again and reduce today's wholly disproportionate influence of the media and those who manipulate the media and the voters alike.

Federalism and Direct Election

Perhaps the most frequent argument made by opponents of direct election is that the electoral college is an important component in preserving the power of the States in our Federal system. Even at the Constitutional Convention, however, the electoral college was not intended to serve that purpose.

The electoral college was effected primarily as a compromise between advocates of popular election such as James Madison, James Wilson and Gouverneur Morris and those who wanted the executive chosen by the legislative branch. The manner of choosing the President was debated sporadically over the summer of 1787, and resolved finally by the contrivance of an appointed Committee of Eleven in the early days of September as a matter of practical politics. It worked well as an arbitration device in 1787 but quickly diminished in utility thereafter.

It is clear that the well-known Great Compromise between large and small states was not a major factor in shaping the electoral college. As Neal Peirce has explained in his book, "The People's President."

> The Great Compromise was devised to settle the dispute over representation in Congress, not the electoral college. It was presented to the Convention on July 5, 1787, and constituted the agreement that made the Federal Union possible. Today it represents a central pillar of the American Federal system which few men have seriously suggested disturbing. . . . At no point in the minutes of the Convention can one find any reference to the application of the Great Compromise to the electoral college's apportionment as important to the Federal system or to the overall structure of the Constitution which was adopted. Indeed, it was never mentioned directly at all. Only in "The Federalist Papers," where James Madison argued at one point that the electoral base for the Presidency would be a "compound" of national and state factors because of the mixed apportionment base, does the argument appear. But no more than indirect reference was made to the apportionment of the electoral college in the State ratifying conventions, or in fact by any of the Nation's leaders until some years after ratification of the Constitution. The argument that the founding fathers viewed the special Federal nature of electoral college apportionment as central to the institution of the Presidency, or to the entire Constitution, is simply false. The small States thought they would gain special advantage, but by another provision— their equal votes in the House in contingent elections.

In the latest hearings on the proposed direct election amendment before the Subcommittee on the Constitution, Professor Emeritus Paul Freund of Harvard addressed the question of whether changing to direct election as a means of electing the President would effect a change on the concept of federalism as conceived by the framers of the Constitution. His reply was that such a change would be much less radical than that of the 17th Amendment in 1913 when we abandoned the indirect election of Senators and thereby abandoned the design of the framers. The original vision of the writers of the Constitution about the selection of the Executive soon proved unworkable. A whole new set of circumstances such as the growth of political parties arose and quickly required the revision of the 12th amendment. What we are proposing with a direct election amendment, according to Professor Freund, would be "to change a revised version of the framers, not the framers' version or vision".

The fundamental tenets of federalism remain today as they did in 1787; the balance between State governments and the Federal Government, and the varying representation in the two Houses of Congress.

Perhaps no better response has been given to the questions about direct election which arise under the name of federalism than that of Senator Mike Mansfield in 1961:

> The Federal system is not strengthened through an antiquated device which has not worked as it was intended to work when it was included in the Constitution and which, if anything, has become a divisive force in the Federal system by pitting groups of States against groups of States. As I see the Federal system in contemporary practice, the House of Representatives is the key to the protection of district interests as to district interests, just as the Senate is the key to the protection of State interests as State interests. These instrumentalities, and particularly the Senate, are the principal constitutional safeguards of the Federal system, but the Presidency has evolved, out of necessity, into the principal political office, as the courts have become the principal legal bulwark beyond districts, beyond States, for safeguarding the interests of all the people in all the States. And since such is the case, in my opinion, the Presidency should be subject to the direct and equal control of all the people.

As Senator Robert Dole remarked in testifying before the Subcommittee for the second time in 1977, direct election serves to enhance real "commonsense" federalism. "Although the electoral college has some of the appearance of our federal system in light of the fact that it is based on a State by State vote, in substance the electoral college may well be more harmful than beneficial to our federal system." Dole explains that with direct election, Presidential candidates would no longer be able to ignore areas in small as well as large States, simply because their supporters are in a clear majority or clear minority. "The voters in the majority of States would receive greater attention and the objectives of federalism would be served better."

Impact of Direct Election on the Smaller States

Just as on the one hand some opponents of direct popular election have argued that it would detract from the power of the voters of larger urban areas and their special interests, other opponents have claimed that it would be disadvantageous to the smaller, less populated States. They have argued that direct election diminishes their voters' power in the electoral college or gives undue weight to the urban States of the Northeast. A careful analysis, however, will show these objections to be ill-founded.

The argument is based upon the fact that the electoral college assigns to each State as many electoral votes as the State has Congressmen and Senators. Since each State has two Senators and at least one Congressman, even if the entire State is far less populated than a single congressional district in a large State, it is argued that smaller States are over-represented in the electoral college. This simple mathematical and theoretical advantage, however, is more than offset by the effects of the unit rule.

Under the unit rule, all of the State's electoral votes are awarded to the candidate who wins a popular vote plurality—regardless of whether the plurality is 1 vote or 1 million votes. The consequence of this "winner-take-all" system is that Presidential campaigns and political power are concentrated in the large, closely contested urban States, where entire State blocs of electoral votes can be won by the narrowest of margins.

Since the vote of an individual voter in the largest electoral vote States has the potential to "swing" all the States' electoral votes, this voter becomes an "advantaged" voter under the electoral college system. This notion has been confirmed by computer analysis and other empirical studies done in recent years by Irwin Mann and Lloyd S. Shapley, John Banzhaf II, John Yunker, Lawrence Longley, and others. All these studies have added mathematical validity to the fact that small States are disfavored by the bias of the electoral college system.

Graphic proof of Presidential candidates' acceptance of the greater relative importance of voters in the largest States was offered during the latest hearings before the subcommittee. The campaign stops of the four major candidates in the fall of 1976 indicate clearly that small States were largely ignored, and large States were visited frequently.

There is little doubt that with direct election, candidates will continue to travel more often to heavily populated areas than sparsely
populated ones. But with direct election, at least communities of the
same size will hold the same attraction whether they are in a large or a
small State.

In addition, according to Douglas Bailey, media manager of the Ford
Dole campaign, the smaller States now largely ignored would receive
additional attention from candidates because with direct election both
the turnout and the plurality become increasingly important.

As Mr. Bailey said,

> The fact of the matter is that while a great deal of the population is
> centered in the urban areas, there is a vast population, with every vote
> counting, that you cannot ignore in a direct election.

Direct Election Would Reduce the Danger of Voter Fraud

According to the minority report from the Committee on the Judiciary in 1970, "One of the most calamitous and probable consequences
of direct popular election will be the increased incidence of election
fraud." The argument is that if fraud occurs under the present system,
the impact is limited to determining the outcome on one State alone.
"The incentive to steal votes is now restricted to close contests in
States which have a sufficiently large electoral vote to alter the final
result. Thus, fraud can be profitable only in a few States, and is seldom
capable of affecting the national outcome."

In reality, the incentive to steal votes "now" as described above is
a fair argument for why the electoral college system itself encourages
fraud. A relatively few irregular votes can reap a healthy reward in the
form of a bloc of electoral votes, because of the unit rule. In short,
under the present system, fraudulent popular votes are likely to have a
greater impact than a like number of fraudulent popular votes under
direct election.

We may cite New York in 1976 as an example. Cries of voting
irregularities arose on election night. At stake were 41 electoral votes—
more than enough to elect Ford over Carter in the electoral college.
Carter's popular margin was 290,000. The calls for recount were
eventually dropped, but if fraud had been present in New York,
Carter's plurality of 290,000 would have been enough to determine the

outcome of the election. Under direct election, at least 1.7 million votes, Carter's national margin, would have had to have been irregular to determine the outcome.

Opponents of direct election charge that a popular vote would increase the incentive for fraud because in a close election every vote would count. It is precisely for this reason that we would have better policing of the polling places by the parties themselves, and possibly even better counting methods and procedural safeguards. The kinds of fraud and voting irregularities which have occurred under the electoral college are frequently in places controlled by one party. And under the electoral college system, there is no incentive for the other party to watch the polls when there is no possibility of carrying the electoral votes.

Critics of Senate Joint Resolution 1 have raised the specter of endless recounts and challenges followed by interminable delay, should direct election be adopted. T. H. White in hearings in 1970 characterized the prospects as a "nightmare." Such dire predictions, however, ignore dangers which now exist under the electoral college, and exaggerate dangers which might arise under direct election.

The opponents' charge is that under direct election, because each vote counts, losing candidates will insist on challenging the result if it is at all a close race. The first response to this alarm is that, as now, a candidate must allege fraud or have some other valid reasons to challenge the vote count. And, as now, he would have to challenge each precinct because that is where counting the votes takes place.

It is commonsense that a candidate will desire a recount only when the candidate perceives that it may change the results in the candidate's favor. And that change of fortune is more likely with the electoral college system than it is with direct election. For example, in 1976, if Ford had carried Ohio and Hawaii he would have gained the electoral majority and would have won the election. A shift of only 9,245 votes in these two States would have accomplished that result. The number of votes nation-wide needed to change the result with a direct election was Carter's plurality of 1.7 million. As L. Kinwin Wroth testified in February, 1977:

> It is sometimes said that the effect of a direct election procedure would be to encourage contests in every precinct. Exactly the converse seems true. Contests are most fruitful to the challenger in a situation like that of 1976 where, under the winner-take-all system, the reversal of one large state's result would mean the capture of the electoral college. Under a

direct election system, President Carter would have had to have lost far more than a few thousand votes in New York and Ohio to lose the election.

Further, recounts will remain unlikely under direct election as they have been with the electoral college system in that experience has shown that overall election recounts generally reveal an almost minuscule shift in number and percent of votes and almost never change the result. Richard Scammon, Director of the Elections Research Center, testified in the latest hearings on direct election,

> Unless you had real corruption at the polls, a specific effort to over-count or undercount for a specific candidate, you normally would expect on the evidence that we have had that the errors tend to cancel each other out and that they are not that serious. . . . We have been putting together for over 20 years now a biennial book of American election statistics and we have never found errors which would have invalidated the whole election.

Critics of direct election, when questioning the recounting procedure, have often described the process in terms of a nationwide project, with the inference that the difficulty and scope of a recount would accordingly be increased. There is nothing in Senate Joint Resolution 1, however, which would change the vote counting procedures from the province of the State. The administrative process of elections in the United States would not be made different by direct election of the President. The voting would take place in all the precincts in the 3,100 counties of the 50 States and the District of Columbia. The administrative problems would not vary in nature from those we now experience with the electoral college system.

This is not to say the counting procedures in this country do not need improvement whether we have direct election or the electoral college system. Institution of direct election might well provide incentive for needed reform. It has been argued, however, that the administrative errors in counting votes is such that in a direct popular election the country would be left in a perpetual state of uncertainty as to whether the candidate receiving the most votes won. Richard Scammon discounts this fear. First of all, there is the consideration that the unit rule of the electoral college system means that a change of a few votes has the potential to change a State's entire bloc of electoral votes. Second, in Mr. Scammon's opinion, the auditing error encountered in elections is one with which we must always deal, and is in no sense fatal. In Mr. Scammon's words:

> [I]t seems to me that what we are speaking about here is an election process that we all live with. Members of this body and the other body, Presidential electors, Presidential candidates, mosquito abatement in a district or whatever it may be, you live with this kind of tolerable error. You meet it as you meet the problems of your automobile by putting oil into the machinery. It has worked very well for us in the past.

It was also Mr. Scammon's opinion that in the event that recounts would be necessary, time would not be an insuperable problem. He estimated that a full count could be gotten nationwide, precinct by precinct, within 2 weeks.

Runoff

The proposed amendment requires the winning candidate to obtain at least 40 percent of the total vote in order to win. Failing that plurality a runoff of the top two candidates is required. The 40 percent figure was arrived at because it was felt necessary to establish a reasonable plurality requirement indicating a legitimate mandate to govern. On the other hand, it was decided that a requirement that was set too high might disrupt the stability of our political system by too easily triggering a runoff.

Contingency plans other than a runoff have been considered previously in committee and on the floor of the Senate during the 1970 debates. The committee retained the runoff provision in Senate Joint Resolution 1 in the belief that in the long run the political health of our democratic system would be better served if the final choice rests with the people. To turn once again to some indirect method of choice such as the Congress to resolve the selection of the President would mean that the choice would be useless if it reflects the will of the people and mischievous if it does not. All the dangers of deals made with third party candidates which now exist with the electoral college would be retained, with no improvement in the means of expressing the wishes of the voters themselves.

A review of Presidential elections shows that the likelihood of a runoff is dim. Only one President, Lincoln, has received less than 40 percent of the popular vote. In 1980 Lincoln received only 39.79

percent of the vote but his name did not appear on the ballot in 10 States.

Further, it appears very unlikely that neither major party candidate would receive a 40 percent plurality—even with a third party candidate in the race. Under the terms of Senate Joint Resolution 1, a splinter party would have to poll at least 20 percent of the total popular vote—and in most instances more—before triggering the runoff. That is considered unlikely in view of the strong two-party system in the United States. In 1968, for example, the most significant third party bid since 1924 could only produce 13.5 percent of the popular vote for George Wallace.

Even more to the point, the committee reviewed the four-way race in 1912, noting that in the face of challenges by an incumbent President and a popular former President, Woodrow Wilson still received more than 40 percent of the popular vote. The four way race in 1948, involving Truman, Dewey, Thurmond, and Wallace, likewise produced a candidate with well over 40 percent of the popular vote. The likelihood of a major party candidate receiving the required plurality, therefore, is not confined merely to third party races but to multiparty contests as well.

The question has been raised as to whether the runoff might not unnecessarily encourage third parties to enter Presidential elections. As analyzed by Prof. Paul Freund of Harvard University before the subcommittee on July 28, 1977, third parties have four motivations to place a candidate in the field. They may hope to win or at least be placed in the runoff; to register the strengths of their movement or cause; to deadlock the election or play a spoiler role; or finally to cause the defeat of a particular major party candidate.

If the motive is to win, the third party obviously must register 40 percent. If it is to place in the runoff, the party must keep both major parties from achieving 40 percent, while at the same time defeating one of the major parties, an extremely difficult task.

If the minor party's aim is to effect a deadlock and exert maximum power in a contingency election, then the electoral college is probably more attractive a system than direct election. To prevent a majority in the electoral vote is far easier for a strong regional candidate than it would be to achieve at least 20 percent of the popular vote while neither major party achieved 40 percent.

Assuming, however, that a minor party candidate or group of candidates is able to garner 20 percent of the popular vote and simultaneously preclude either major party candidate from receiving at least 40 percent of the remaining votes, the bargaining position obtained may be less than would at first appear. The ability of the candidate to control the votes of all those individuals who once claimed to support him is not tantamount to the influence held by a candidate over electors pledged to that candidate. Thus, it is unlikely that a minor party candidate will be able to deliver all the votes of his supporters, even if he endorses one of the major party candidates. Moreover, once the 20 percent ceases to represent a unified coalition, the bargaining power of the minor party candidates decreases substantially.

Racial and Minority Group Voting Power Under Electoral College and Direct Election Systems

Some have defended the present electoral college approach on the theory that the system as it operates gives disproportionate voting influence to racial or ethnic minorities, thereby offsetting some of the economic or social deprivations historically suffered by these groups. The late Prof. Alexander M. Bickel of Yale Law School was a major proponent of this view. In hearings before the Senate Judiciary Committee in 1970 during a previous consideration of electoral reform he stated,

> The system is, therefore, in effect malapportioned in favor of the large industrial States, in which party competition is vigorous, and which generally swing by small percentages of the popular vote. Not only that but the system is in effect malapportioned in favor of cohesive interest, ethnic or racial groups within these States, which often go nearly in block for a candidate, and can swing the State and its entire electoral vote.

This conclusion in respect to racial groups has been undermined in recent years, however, by empirical analyses which have been done of voting power under the electoral college. Working from their computer studies, for example, Lawrence Longley and John Yunker calculate that a black voter on the average has 2.4 percent less voting power with the electoral college than the average American voter. And in a separate, unpublished study by Douglas H. Blair of the University of Pennsylvania, the following conclusion was reached:

> The empirical findings of this essay suggest that suburban native whites, the most economically advantaged of the nine demographic groups also wield the most political power in the selection of the President under either of two power measures. They further indicate that this power

would be diminished by abolition of the electoral college. Blacks, on the
other hand, the least economically advantaged of the groups, are shown
to have below average voting power under the electoral college procedure
according to each index; they would gain power under direct election. It
would seem to be no very strenuous normative leap, for an egalitarian to
the conclusion that electoral reform is in order.

The belief that the electoral college system benefits racial or ethnic
minorities in large urban areas is heavily based on the assumption that
these population centers are located in heavily populated States and
that Presidential candidates are attracted to these areas because they
command large numbers of electoral votes. The underlying assumption
regarding the population distribution of racial minorities is questionable, however. Census figures show that blacks are not in fact congre-
gated in the most heavily populated States, at least as much as whites
are. The six "big" States, in terms of population and electoral votes,
are Ohio, Illinois, Texas, Pennsylvania, New York, and California.
Among them they control 190 electoral votes. They as a whole contain
40.8 percent of the Nation's population. As for the Nation's blacks,
however, only 37.1 percent live in these so-called swing States. These
figures give credence to the conclusion of Lawrence Longley, Douglas
Blair, William J. D. Boyd, H. Zeidenstein and others that blacks as a
whole are "disadvantaged" voters under the electoral college system.
They simply do not live in the heavily advantaged States in the
proportion that whites do.

Another census figure should be noted that is frequently overlooked
in the analysis of minorities' votes with the electoral college. The fact
is that more blacks than whites are rural dwellers; 4 to 5 percent of the
national population is classified as "rural"—18 percent of blacks,
however, live in "rural" areas, according to the U.S. census.

Even if we were to assume for the sake of argument, however,
that racial minorities were centered in heavily populated States, any
possible "benefit" that the electoral college system would confer over
the direct election would be more apparent than real. Several fallacies
of the theory of electoral college benefit to racial and other minorities
should be brought out.

First, while it is correct, of course, that large States are more
politically powerful because they can deliver more electoral votes, it is
also evident that under a direct election approach areas of the country
with large populations will continue to draw significant candidate
attention simply because of the number of potential voters gathered

there. Whatever alleged disproportionate influence exists under the present system as a result of the large numbers of electoral votes that are clustered in States where minority groups are also located, will certainly continue under direct election since candidates tend to concentrate on areas which control the greatest numbers of potential votes.

Perhaps the one aspect of the electoral college system which carries with it the greatest burden for ethnic or racial minorities is the unit rule provision. This system, which awards all of a State's electoral votes to the candidate who wins a majority of the popular vote, can have an impact on minority voting strength that is little short of devastating.

The nature of the unit rule provision carries with it the very real potential to erase the views of the minority voter while magnifying the strength of the majority voter. For example, black voting percentages for Mr. Carter were 94.5 percent in Indiana, 95.2 percent in Michigan and 94.7 percent in Virginia, States which went to Mr. Ford. All of these black Democratic votes were lost under the electoral college system. In fact, it might be said that those black votes for Carter were actually recast for Ford under the present winner-take-all unit rule.

This effect of the unit rule is particularly devastating to ethnic or racial minorities which often share common political goals and interests throughout the country. Under the present electoral college system their votes are "washed out" in unsuccessful winner-take-all State-by-State contests rather than being pooled with other ethnic or minority group votes as would be possible under a direct election system. As Neal R. Pierce has noted in his book, "The People's President," on the question of whether ethnic or minority group members would lose voting power under a direct election system:

> The answer is clearly no . . . They would be able to transfer their voting strength to the national stage instead—and be just as effective there . . . Negroes from Southern States like Georgia and Alabama would be able to combine their Presidential votes with Negroes from New York, Illinois and Michigan and thus constitute a formidable national voting bloc that the parties would ignore at their peril.

Similarly, even when minority and ethnic group voters support the winning candidate in a particular State they also may find numbers of their votes "wasted." For example, the Joint Center for Political Studies revealed that there were large blocks of black votes in the

Carter States of Georgia, Massachusetts, New York, Arkansas, Tennessee, North Carolina, Florida, Alabama, Texas, Pennsylvania, South Carolina, Louisiana, Maryland, and the District of Columbia. The total plurality for Carter in those States and the District of Columbia amounted to 2,751,345 votes. Thus, almost 2.8 million votes were wasted in the electoral college. They generated no more electoral votes than would have resulted from a plurality of only 14 votes, one in each State and the District of Columbia.

Essentially, the direct election approach is the only method of insuring that minority and ethnic group voters across the country exercise the voting power which their numbers command. Under the present system this voting power is in constant danger of being erased in losing States or wasted in winning States. Direct election would for the first time allow ethnic or minority voters to join together and speak with a voice commensurate with their role in American society.

A final question is answered by direct election, and that is the question of fundamental fairness. With direct election every vote would count. Every vote would count the same, urban or rural, black or white, rich or poor; north, south, east or west. And the person with the most votes would win. Only direct election accomplishes this result.

One of the most eloquent supporters of direct election in the House of Representatives is Congressman John Conyers of Detroit. As Congressman Conyers argued on the floor of the House in 1969:

> To advocate a direct popular election of the President, as outlined in House Joint Resolution 681, was not an especially easy decision for me to make. As a black Representative from a populous State with a significant block of black voters, I have considered the arguments that a direct election would deprive my constituents, especially my black constituents, of an advantage they now possess under the electoral system. . . . But there are other facets of this problem, and I am impressed by their significance. The one man, one vote rule has effectively enfranchised black Americans and other minority group members in voting for Congress. In a similar way, the direct election of the President will effectively enfranchise black Americans and others where they now may vote, but where their vote does not really count.
>
> The direct election of our President will insure that a black man's vote will count in those States where it is currently ineffectual, will mean that the people will vote for the President as a citizen of the United States rather than a citizen of a State, and will allow the vote of each person— black or white to carry equal weight.

* * *

Only with the adoption of the direct popular election can the minority residents of America look forward to the day when he is just as free as is his white counterpart to vote for the candidate of his choice, and without race emerging as a primary consideration.

* * *

I feel that the advantages of a direct popular vote for President for all Americans are clear. The advantage to our Nation's minority residents is an opportunity for them to possess a full and equal share in the democratic process by which this Nation is governed, and by which so many of its wrongs can be righted.

Conclusion

For the foregoing reasons, the Committee on the Judiciary recommends prompt enactment of the subject resolution.

Cost Estimate Pursuant to Section 252 of the Legislative Reorganization Act of 1970

Pursuant to section 252(a) of the Legislative Reorganization Act of 1970 (Public Law 91–510), the committee estimates that there will be no costs to the Federal Government resulting from passage of this resolution.

Tabulation of Votes Cast in Committee

Pursuant to section 133(b) of the Legislative Reorganization Act of 1946, as amended by Public Law 91–510, the following is a tabulation of votes in committee:

Morton to report Senate Joint Resolution 1 to the Senate was approved by a vote of 9 to 8 as follows:

YEA	NAY
Kennedy	Eastland
Bayh	McClellan
Byrd	Allen
Abourezk	Thurmond
Biden	Scott
Culver	Laxalt
Metzenbaum	Hatch
DeConcini	Wallop
Mathias	

Minority Views of Messrs. Eastland, Allen, Thurmond, Scott, Laxalt, Hatch, and Wallop on S.J. Res. 1

Contents

Introduction.
Danger of applying "one-man, one-vote" to the Presidency.
Reasonable majorities.
Direct election could destroy the party system.
The need for broadly based parties.
Direct election would encourage splinter parties.
Dangers of the run-off.
Direct election would reduce State political base.
Media influence on direct election.
Direct election would undermine the separation of powers.
Direct election would radicalize American public opinion.
Direct election would undermine moderate influence.
Direct election would endanger minority rights.
Direct election would encourage challenges and recounts.
The third party phenomenon.
Conclusion.

Introduction

We believe that the committee majority of 9 to 8, has embraced a scheme that will adversely affect the entire constitutional and political structure of the United States.

Direct election of the President, in our opinion would:

Remove the States as factors in the Presidential election process thus crippling federalism.

Increase the chances of a candidate who received less than 50 percent of the popular vote being elected to office.

Lead to electoral recounts and challenges.

Increase national control of the electoral process.

Give undue weight to numbers—thus further reducing the influence of the smaller States.

Bring about drastic changes in the strategy and tactics used in campaigns for the Presidency; encourage simplistic media-oriented campaigns, and reduce personal campaigning outside of large metropolitan areas.

Encourage candidates for President representing narrow geographical, ideological, and ethnic bases of support rather than the broad coalitions represented by major party candidates.

Increase the power of big city political bosses.

Increase the likelihood of voter fraud in Presidential elections.

The undersigned oppose direct election of the President and Vice President. Some favor no change, others would prefer the proportional system or the district plan. All are opposed to Senate Joint Resolution 1.

Danger of Applying "One-Man, One-Vote" to the Presidency

Nothing could be clearer in the Framers' thoughts than their rejection of a merely numerical concept of representative Government. This is true of the federal system, which among other things, prevents the less populous States from being engulfed by the more populous States; this is true of bicameralism, which divides legislative responsibilities between House and Senate on grounds other than those of population; this is true of the separation of powers, whereby great power is invested in a nonelective judiciary; and this is true of the electoral college, which incorporates the Federal principle and grants to each State, however small, a minimum weight of three electoral votes.

Reasonable Majorities

The departures from strict mathematical equality were designed to prevent any group, whether a minority or a majority, from seriously or permanently interfering with the rights of others.

Since the Constitution is dedicated to securing equal rights for all, it follows that only those majorities are entitled to rule which respect the rights of those who do not agree with them. The Constitution is equally devoted to majority rule and minority rights. The central character of American politics requires that we be concerned not just with the size of majorities but with their character. It should be noted that under the present system the popular vote prevails. The difference, of course, being that the votes are counted within the respective States rather than having a national tabulation.

The crucial question in considering electoral reform is whether one method of election is better than another at creating reasonable majorities. One method might be better at obtaining a strictly numerical majority, but only at the price of failing to protect minorities; another might protect minorities, but only at the price of frustrating a truly reasonable majority.

In Presidential elections, which are politically and symbolically the most important elections in the country, the present system attempts to create numerical majorities which are moderate in character. It does this in part by granting a certain weight to numbers—hence greater representation for the more populous States. The electoral system—

Supports the federal system by giving the States as States a say in the selection and election of Presidents;

Encourages compromise among antagonistic interests by seeing to it that compromises are worked out well in advance of elections and within geographically limited political areas;

Permits the representation of certain interests whose only drawback is the want of great numbers; and

Places institutional restraints upon the abuse of powers in the Chief Executive Office.

In short, it brings together all the distinctive elements of the American Constitution and provides indispensable institutional support for the federal system and the separation of powers. It has through the years become inextricably intertwined with the two-party system and the national conventions which carry out the Constitution's dedication to reasonable majorities in the everyday political process.

Direct Election Could Destroy the Party System

It is generally agreed that our two-party system has been an indispensable aid in carrying out the dual purpose of American politics: majority rule with minority rights. It is also generally agreed that in a multiparty system either or both of these goals would be frustrated. Given the extent and variety of interests which compose this land, the maintenance of a two-party system is a remarkable feat. Indeed, the striking fact about American party politics is not that we have had a number of third-party movements, but that we have not had more of them. All third-party movements in U.S. history, taken together, account for only 5 percent of the total vote cast in Presidential elections.

The two-party system is not a product of chance. Public opinion has no inherent tendency to divide itself into two, and only two, major political groupings. The ultimate causes of two-party politics are to be found in the requirements of the Presidential election system under which parties have operated for nearly a century and a half.

From the moment of their inception, the major parties as we know them, had as their central organizing purpose the capturing of the Presidency. In order to carry out that goal, the parties had to contend with four constitutional requirements—a unitary Presidency; the necessity of carrying a majority of electoral votes; the distribution of electoral votes according to States; and the awarding of electoral votes within the States on the basis of winner-take-all. These factors are chiefly responsible for the most distinctive features of the American party system:

1. We have only two major parties—third party movements have been sporadic and, on the whole, ineffectual.

2. The major parties, often called "national" are in fact coalitions of 50 State parties which, in turn, are coalitions of county and local party organizations.

3. Both major parties include a wide range of interests and a broad spectrum of opinion.

The Need for Broadly Based Parties

Because a majority of electoral votes is required for victory, a party seeking the Presidency must expand its base of support beyond a narrow geographical region. And because electoral votes are apportioned according to the Federal principle, a party must campaign in all or most of the States. The States, thus, are the decisive political battlegrounds. The States, of course, are free to award their electoral votes as they see it. All States, except Maine, follow the practice of awarding electoral votes by the unit rule, winner-take-all; and they have followed the practice without notable exception for 150 years.

Winner-take-all encourages both parties to include everyone and to exclude no one. Both have traditional bases of support which remain loyal over a considerable period of time; but with rare exceptions, these are seldom sufficient to provide the margin of victory. In most States, most of the time, neither party can afford to alienate any sizable interest group; both are forced to seek the support of those who are not traditionally wedded to either party. Since both parties face the same requirements in all States, an electoral majority, when it does emerge, is both geographically dispersed and ideologically moderate. The victorious party is therefore capable of governing. The electoral college, in sum, produces truly competitive, State-based, moderate political parties. Moderate national parties also operate to confine third parties to a narrow regional base.

Direct Election Would Encourage Splinter Parties

Under direct election, most of the incentives toward moderate broadly based, two party competition would be removed. While it is

true that a sizable plurality—40 percent—would be required for victory, that alone is not sufficient to sustain two-party competition as we
have known. Under direct election it is not the distribution of the vote
which matters, but only its size. Votes would be sought without regard
to the States which happened to contain them. Interest groups would
face no necessity to moderate their views or to compromise with other
groups within their resident States; and candidates would face no
necessity to present a broadly based platform within each State.

The direct election proposal makes no provision whatsoever for
any pre-election machinery capable of putting together a 40 percent
coalition, or of insuring that the coalition will be truly representative
of the Nation as a whole. The proponents of direct election assume
that all else in the political process will go on pretty much as-is, that
the negotiation, compromise, and coalition now undertaken by the two
major parties with the States will be performed in the same way.
Needless to say, we have strong reservations about that prospect.

Dangers of the Runoff

Our reservations about direct election in general are in every respect
strengthened when we come to consider the run-off provision. Some
proponents of direct election have expressed concern that the run-off
provision of S.J. Res. 1 would encourage splinter party candidacies
and therefore make it impossible for anyone to obtain 40 percent in the
first election. They suggest that elimination of the run-off would
insulate direct election against the threat of party proliferation. Nevertheless, the elimination of the run-off is only a partial solution to the
problem of splinter parties. It would discourage some, but by no means
all, troublesome minor party candidates; but it would have little effect
on so-called spoiler candidates—those who run, not to win, but to
prevent someone else from winning.

The only way to guarantee that someone will be able to garner at
least 40 percent of the vote under direct election is to limit sharply the
number of candidates in a race. Without rigid, universally applicable
rules narrowing the field of candidates, the "spoiler" strategy may still
be profitably pursued under direct election even if the runoff provision
is removed.

The form and content of existing laws governing party and candidate
eligibility differ widely from State to State. Under direct election,
however, this diversity might produce a sufficient number of minor
candidacies to prevent a major candidate from obtaining at least 40

percent of the vote. A uniform Federal rule on candidate eligibility might also be necessary. If so, Congress would have to pass and enforce laws covering all the matters now regulated by State law, and the myriad functions now undertaken by fifty secretaries of state will have to be performed by a single national authority.

Direct Election Would Reduce State Political Base

One of the distinctive features of the American party system is that our parties are essentially State-dominated. The major parties are organized from the grassroots up—a feature which enables them to accommodate a wide diversity of competing interests at the State and local level, and helps to keep elected officials responsive to State and local needs. What brings the thousands of State and local party units together is the attempt, every four years to capture the Presidency.

The most obvious symbol of the State orientation of the major parties is the national convention. Delegates come to the conventions as representatives of their States and voting power is allocated in proportion to electoral vote strength. Direct election would destroy the utility of having delegates selected, or votes distributed in this matter. It is doubtful, indeed, whether there would be conventions at all under direct election. The logic of direct election leads inexorably toward Presidential primaries, perhaps regional but most likely national in scope.

It is apparent that the role of the States in the electoral college contributes greatly to national stability and is necessary for the cohesion of State party organizations. The importance of cohesion in State party organizations is obvious. In most States, most of the time, a single party organization is able to coordinate Presidential, gubernatorial, senatorial, congressional, and other campaigns, and can thus act as a mediator among the conflicting aims of politicians and interest groups. Once the States as States are removed from the Presidential election process, a strong inducement toward State party cohesion will also be removed. Therefore, a significant restructuring of State and national party organizations would take place, which in turn, could alter in unforeseen ways the power of the States to carry on political business, especially in relation to the National Government. We simply do not know with any precision how much of a Governor's or a Senator's or a Congressman's power derives from his State's role in the electoral system. We may be certain, however, that it is often considerable, and that Presidents are influenced by it.

Media Influence on Direct Election

Testimony received at recent hearings would indicate that, in contrast to the conclusion of the majority, direct election would encourage the trend toward centralized campaigns for the Presidency. During the course of that testimony the head of a media agency stated that a system of direct election of the President would involve at least three adverse changes: The substitution of media marketing for political planning; campaigns that would reflect national opinion polls rather than special interests of regions and States; and the demise of State and local political organizations.

Furthermore, a member of the Judiciary Committee expressed the fear that the effect of direct elections would be that a large part of America would never again witness an election campaign for a President. Those outside of American urban areas would not see future Presidential candidates.

Direct Election Would Undermine the Separation of Powers

One of the least discussed but most dangerous aspects of direct election is its tendency to undo the delicate balance among the three branches of the National Government.

Separation of powers is rightly and most commonly thought of as referring to the distribution of functions among the executive, legislative and judicial branches; but the manner of that distribution exists in part by virtue of the balance which was struck between the States and the National Government.

Among the considerations weighed by the Framers in designing the Presidency was the desirability of providing the President with a constituency essentially independent from that of Congress and that of the States.

The purpose of an independent constituency is to give energy to the executive, to avoid that disunity and frustration which might arise if the President were overly indebted to Congress or to the States for his election or reelection. But there was an equally strong desire to prevent the President from abusing the great powers of his office. This latter desire was carried out, first, by involving the States in the election process; and second, by distributing governmental powers at the national level, chiefly as between the two dominant branches. In practice, the balance of power between the executive and legislative branches has sometimes rested with the White House, sometimes with Congress, and most frequently, somewhere in between.

Under direct election, there is a strong likelihood that the entire constitutional balance will come undone for there is more to the relationship between President and Congress than the formal separation of powers on paper will ever reveal. Insofar as the future under direct election can be foreseen at all, it is clear that there will be a radical restructuring of State and national party organizations. Once the States as States are excluded from the Presidential election process, the subsequent restructuring of State and national party organizations will necessarily affect Members of Congress both in their capacity as representative of their States and in their individual and collective relations with the President. Congress has been accustomed to deal with a President who is in part dependent upon, and therefore restrained by, the States. A President who is independent of the States, and whose political obligations bear no predictable relations to existing party organizations, may be an entirely different creature.

Direct Election Would Radicalize American Public Opinion

The central political goal of the Constitution in general and the electoral college in particular is the creation of reasonable majorities, that is, of majorities which will not prey upon the rights of others. The Constitution and the electoral college seek to accomplish this task by providing salutary incentives to compromise by rewarding moderation and penalizing extremism. This process requires for its effectuation a blurring rather than an accentuation of the differences among men. The genius of our present method of election may be said to consist precisely in its ability to reveal what men have in common and to conceal what they do not.

Direct Election Would Undermine Moderate Influence

The creation of a reasonable majority in a country of this size and diversity is a task of enormous magnitude. The number and variety of interests are such that any majority must necessarily be a coalition of minorities, each of which, quite naturally, tends to prefer its own interest to those of others. The peculiar merit of our present system is precisely that it forces every group to see the satisfaction of its own interest as depending in large part on the satisfaction of other interests. But the majority which merges from the coalition of essentially self-interested minorities retains the character of its parts, which is to say that a majority is only temporarily harmonious. A majority within each major party is constantly in tension, with the result that a party's capacity to command the allegiance of its followers, in power or out, is constantly being challenged. A coalition which wins at one election may not win at the next—a fact which induces party leaders and Presidents to seek new bases of support and to be wary of alienating any significant group presently loyal to their party.

The electoral system says, in effect, that so long as Presidents are going to be indebted to certain interests for their election or for their reelection, it is better to have those interests funneled through the mediating influence of the States. The States as members of a Federal union ought properly to be represented as States in the Presidency.

Direct Election Would Endanger Minority Rights

So successful has the electoral system been that most Americans are inclined to forget that they are, in one or more senses, members of a minority—geographic, ethnic, religious, social, or economic. Under our present system, to be a member of the losing party carries no long-term liability; it neither invites invidious discrimination nor endangers the security of one's liberty. We are therefore inclined to think of minorities in terms of others, as those proverbial "other fellows." Nonetheless, the fact remains that each of us is a member of a potentially vulnerable minority. What is true of one minority will, sooner or later be true of every other. This fact has been obscured by the very success of the electoral college in putting together widely dispersed and virtually all-inclusive pluralities. But the significance of being a member of one or more minorities, might be much greater under a different system of election, especially direct election. One's fundamental rights may very well be affected by whether or not he is a member of the winning coalition.

The power of all minorities comes from the skill with which they are able to join themselves to other minorities. It is a string of such minorities which constitutes a majority or a winning plurality. A minority which fails to align itself with other minorities is a minority which finds its political power greatly diminished. One of the chief virtues of the electoral college is that it not only encourages such alliances, but virtually requires them. It builds moderate majorities while protecting the interests of all minorities that are willing to compromise.

Under direct election, with its emphasis on mere numbers, the strength of most so-called minorities, especially those which lack significant numbers, would likely be diminished. Under our two-party system, which is held together by the electoral system, those minorities which are not permanently wedded to one party have an opportunity to switch their support with maximum effect; for the loss to one is compounded by a gain for the other.

Therefore, the multiplication of parties, the removal of the States from the electoral process, and the other inducements toward extremism that would result from direct election—all these factors would diminish the power of minorities.

Direct Election Would Encourage Challenges and Recounts

One of the most serious threats to our national stability under direct election would be the probability of contested elections. A contested election under any system is certainly dangerous.

Under the present system, the popular vote in most States, most of the time, is insulated against challenge and recount. Only extremely close and bitter contests in certain strategic States would ever tempt one of the major parties to call for a recount in a Presidential contest. Under direct election, however, the popular vote in every State would be open to the perpetual threat of challenge. Whether a candidate wins or loses a State by a large or small margin of votes, recounted votes in that State under direct election could still affect the national result.

The uncertainties surrounding a recount to determine the outcome of a close Presidential election could paralyze our Nation. Even the mechanical aspects of a sizable recount would be dangerous enough, but if legal questions concerning voter qualifications and other matters were to be raised, as they surely would be, the period of the recount would be nothing short of chaotic. It is clear that recounts will be a disastrous problem for the United States should direct election of the President become law.

The Third Party Phenomenon

Assaults against the electoral system seem to escalate in number and intensity during or just after close election campaigns, or in years when a third party candidate has made inroads into traditional major-party areas. Most commonly, the hue and cry for reform comes from the ranks of the party which has just lost or fears it is about to lose the White House, or from that party which is most adversely affected by the third-party movement.

We submit, however, that the electoral system far from making it possible for a third party to precipitate a constitutional crisis, in point of fact has prevented just such a crisis from taking place. The decisive question is what actually happened to prior third party candidates? In spite of their intentions, third party Presidential efforts have been necessarily confined to a narrow sectional base. They have been confined to a narrow sectional base precisely because the electoral college requires that a successful Presidential campaign be conducted in all or most of the States, which requires, in turn, that a candidate make a broadly based appeal to the voters. Moreover, because of the strong two-party structure, many would-be party supporters have been induced to cast their ballots for one of the major party candidates.

Conclusion

In summary, we believe that the proposal should be rejected for the following reasons:
It would cripple the party system and encourage splinter parties;
It would undermine the federal system;
It would alter the delicate balance underlying separation of powers;
It would encourage electoral fraud;
It could lead to interminable recounts and challenges;
It would necessitate national control of every aspect of the electoral process;
It would give undue weight to numbers; thereby reducing the influence of small states;
It would encourage candidates for President to represent narrow geographical, ideological, and ethnic bases of support;
It would encourage simplistic media-oriented campaigns and bring about drastic changes in the strategy and tactics used in campaigns for the Presidency; and
It would increase the power of big city political bosses.
Fair minded persons must admit that over the years, our present electoral system, in conjunction with the party system which grew up in response to it, for the most part, has produced independent, responsible Chief Executives.

JAMES O. EASTLAND.
JAMES B. ALLEN.
STROM THURMOND.
WILLIAM L. SCOTT.
PAUL LAXALT.
ORRIN G. HATCH.
MALCOLM WALLOP.

• • •

Additional Views of Mr. Hatch

Changing the fundamental nature of our Constitution is an awesome undertaking that should be approached with extreme caution. Changing it radically—and that is precisely what Senate Joint Resolution 1 seeks to accomplish—is a dangerous undertaking that may prove fatal. Changing it when there is no compelling reason to justify the change is thus not only unnecessary but risky. In other words, when it is not necessary to change the Constitution, it is necessary not to change it.

The electoral college, in spite of its faults, has served us well for two centuries. The burden of proof rests with the proponents of Senate Joint Resolution 1 to show that their electoral scheme is better and safer than the present system. My study of the testimony, the leading works on the subject, and the committee report, leads me inexorably to the conclusion that the "reformers" have simply not proved their case. In addition, the testimony of three eminent political scientists who appeared before the Constitution Subcommittee—Martin Diamond, Herbert Storing, and Judith Best, author of "The Case Against Direct Election of the President," indicates that the supporters of this pernicious amendment are laboring under a profound misunderstanding of our constitutional system.

The indictment against the Electoral College hinges on four propositions, three of which are said to constitute "dangerous" imperfections in our system. But "all the dangers critics claim to see in the electoral college," observes Diamond, "are entirely matters of speculation. Some have never actually occurred, and others have not occurred for nearly a century. Nothing whatever has actually gone wrong with the electoral college for a very long time. Experience has demonstrated that the dangers incident to the present system are neither grave nor likely to occur."

Tempests in Teacups

What are these so-called "dangers"? The committee report calls our attention first to the problem of the "dangerous anachronistic elector." According to this line of reasoning, "The prospect of unknown electors auctioning off the Presidency to the highest bidder, is all too real."

One wonders, however, whether the "faithless elector" is really a serious problem. Authorities estimate that there have been no more than ten of these out of about 20,000 electoral ballots cast. In no instance have they exerted any influence on the final election result. Their perfidy may offend our democratic sensibilities, but their existence is irrelevant.

Even if we assume that this handful of "faithless electors" threatens the integrity of our system, it does not necessarily follow that the complete elimination of the elector is the best solution. "Perhaps the office of elector would have some utility," observes Best, "if electors were national party professionals rather than nonentities—no contingency plan suggested to date is clearly satisfactory, and this proposal is no exception. But even if one believes that it is undesirable to continue the office of elector, the problem of faithless electors is minuscule, and the meager and technical benefits of eliminating the office do not justify the effort to pass a constitutional amendment."

The second charge in the indictment against the electoral college is equally chimerical. According to the committee report, "the present system can elect a President who has fewer popular votes than his opponent and thus is not the first choice of the voters." Peering into the future, the report insists that "The most dangerous result of the unit rule of our present electoral system is the lack of guarantee that the candidate with the most popular votes will win. This dangerous prospect, more than anything else, condemns the present system as an imperfect device for recording the sentiment of American voters."

This is an overstatement which collapses under the stress of objective analysis. Mathematically, of course, it is possible for a minority candidate to be elected President. But what has been the case when we look at actual practice rather than the crystal ball? The Report claims that "In 1824, 1876, and again in 1888 this system produced Presidents who were not the popular choice of the voters." This, too, is an overstatement. In the 1824 election, it is true that John Quincy Adams was elected by the House, even though Andrew Jackson enjoyed a popular plurality of approximately 37,000 votes. It must be remembered, however, that there were four candidates in that election, and no one received a majority of the electoral votes. In six states, with 71 electoral votes or 27 percent of the total, the electors were chosen not by the people but by the State legislatures. There is no way, then, as Professor Best correctly observes, "to determine the total popular vote in 1824, and therefore no way to conclude that Jackson was deprived of a popular victory."

Likewise, the election of Hayes in 1876 does not present a convincing example of a runner-up President. As Best has noted, "Although the statistical histories give Tilden the plurality over Hayes in the election of 1876, it is difficult to assert with any confidence that he actually surpassed Hayes in the popular vote, since both sides engaged in widespread fraud in casting and counting the votes."

This leaves us with the Harrison election of 1888, the only instance where the electoral college clearly and unequivocally produced a runner-up President. Grover Cleveland, winner of the popular vote, was defeated by Benjamin Harrison, who captured the electoral vote. But there is no indication that this unique event undermined public confidence in the American system, or produced any of the terrible results that have been conjured up by the advocates of direct election. Here, in bold relief, is the principal danger that the reformers fear. As Diamond puts it, "This is the loaded pistol pointed to our heads, the threat that necessitates radical constitutional revision. Now the funny thing about this loaded pistol is that the last time it went off, in 1888, no one got hurt; no one even hollered. As far as I can tell, there was hardly a ripple of constitutional discontent, not a trace of dangerous delegitimation, and nothing remotely resembling the crisis predicted by present-day critics of the electoral college."

Nearly a century has elapsed since the peculiar election of a runner-up President in 1888. This can be hardly seen as indicative that the electoral college is chronically defective. Are the American people capable of enduring another minority President at some future time if the system fails to live up to expectations? There is no way of knowing for certain how they would react. Recent experience with the 25th amendment and the "election" of Gerald Ford strongly suggests, however, that our fellow countrymen are more resilient than the reformers would allow, and more concerned about the legitimacy of the process than its obeisance to an absolute standard of majoritarianism. In any event, a single aberration does not justify a wholesale destruction of a workable system, any more than an isolated departure from our established norm of justice would warrant the burning of the courthouse.

The third indictment against our time-honored method of electing the President is an extension of the runner-up problem that fizzled in 1888. But this time we step off the platform of reality and enter the world of speculation, conjecture, and game theory. "On numerous occasions," states the committee report, "a shift of less than 1 percent of the popular vote would have produced an electoral majority for the candidate who received fewer popular votes. In 1948, for example a shift of less than 30,000 popular votes in 3 States would have given

Governor Dewey an electoral vote majority—despite President Truman's 2 million-plus popular vote margin.''

Admittedly, the possibilities here for changing the election results by juggling the figures are infinite, and I observe that the supporters of Senate Joint Resolution 1 have even brought in computers to demonstrate the myriad ways in which popularly supported Presidents can be transformed into second best has-beens. What all of these calculations prove I am not quite sure, except that computers are useless when it comes to judging the merits of a complex political institution. Computers cannot tell us what is noble or just, heroic or cowardly, any more than they can tell us what is the value of our electoral college.

National Majoritarianism versus Federal Democracy

So much, then, for the alleged "dangers" of our electoral college. Much has been written on the other side of the ledger about the dangers incident to the direct election proposal, so I shall not dwell upon them at length. Suffice to say that "the most dangerous" feature of the present system, to quote the reformers, is no less a problem under Senate Joint Resolution 1. The electoral college, says the reformers, is evil because it permits the election of a minority candidate. But doesn't the provision of Senate Joint Resolution 1 allowing for the election of the 40 percent plus candidate create the same difficulty? The proponents of Senate Joint Resolution 1 fail to answer this question satisfactorily.

But let's not quibble over speculative matters. What's really at stake here is the survival of our system of government. This resolution, along with a number of other proposals now pending before Congress, represents a concerted effort on the part of a number of Members to impose upon our Constitution a philosophy of democracy that is wholly alien to our constitutional heritage and system of free government. I view this development with alarm, and I firmly believe that it should be vigorously resisted.

At the heart of Senate Joint Resolution 1 is the assumption that our electoral college is faulty because it is "undemocratic." This is so, argue the reformers, because it permits the election of a runner-up President. It is "the most dangerous" feature of our electoral system, they say. What is more, the unit rule or "winner-take-all" formula disfranchises voters who supported the losing candidate in their State because the entire electoral vote is awarded to the candidate they opposed. The system must be condemned, says the committee report, because it creates an "obvious injustice."

But it is equally obvious that the philosophy of democracy inherent in these allegations is not the American philosophy of democracy. It goes by another name. Some call it total democracy; others call it majoritarianism, plebiscitary democracy, or populism. Be that as it may, the important point to bear in mind is that this philosophy of democracy was considered and wisely rejected by the Framers of our Constitution. It was rejected because it runs counter to our political character and weakens the barriers against despotism.

Perhaps the reformers would put away their guns if they were aware that the underlying philosophy of democracy which impels them to shoot up the electoral college also requires, by the force of their reasoning, that they attack our whole system of representation; for their logic puts them at odds with any and all district forms of elections. Popular votes for the Senate are federally aggregated on a State basis, and every State has the same number of Senators in spite of population inequalities. It necessarily follows that a discrepancy between the national popular vote and control of the Senate is likely to occur. Indeed, we can go further and point to the inequalities that exist between the voters of a State with a small population and those with a large one. This is also true of the House of Representatives, but to a lesser extent, because every State is entitled to at least one Representative, irrespective of its population size.

Despite the claims of the reformers that these departures from pure democracy are "unjust," "dangerous," and "undemocratic," it is obvious that this is not the way the American people see it. They understand, if the reformers do not, that there are other factors to consider besides a simplistic counting of heads. As Martin Diamond has explained, "Americans have always believed that there is more to democracy itself than merely maximizing national majoritarianism; our idea of democracy includes responsiveness to local majorities as well. Further, because of our multiplicity of interests, ethnic groups, religions, and races, we have always believed in local democratic responsiveness to geographically based minorities whose interests may otherwise be utterly neglected; such minorities secure vigorous direct representation, for example, only because of the districted basis of the House of Representatives. The State-by-State responsiveness of the electoral college is an equally legitimate form of districted, local democratic responsiveness. In short, in the case of both the House and Senate, we accept the risk (and the occasional reality) of the national popular-vote/district vote discrepancy because the advantages to be gained are great and because the House and Senate remain nationally democratic enough to satisfy any reasonable standard of democracy.''

Diamond's acute observations reflect the genius of American democracy: attention to local as well as national democratic considerations. He puts the electoral college in its proper democratic perspective thusly: ''The label given to the proposed reform, 'direct popular election,' is a misnomer; the elections have already become as directly popular as they can be—but in the States. Despite all their democratic rhetoric, the reformers do not propose to make our presidential elections more directly democratic, they only propose to make them directly national, by entirely removing the states from the electoral process. Democracy thus is not the question regarding the electoral college, federalism is: should our Presidential elections remain in part federally democratic, or should we make them completely nationally democratic? Whatever we decide, then, democracy itself is not at stake in our decision, only the prudential question of how to channel and organize the popular will.''

In sum, the electoral college, like the Constitution itself, embodies the democratic spirit and the American practice of channeling and moderating democracy through a complex arrangement that is responsive to all democratic considerations, and not just the numerical. All of our elections, including the Presidential, are freely and democratically contested—but in the States. I see nothing to be gained, and much to be lost, by abandoning a proven method of election that has adapted to every change and development in the political history of this country merely for the sake of an abstract and discredited notion of popular government. An unrestrained and undifferentiated national democracy may satisfy the passions of our reformers, but it will never satisfy the public good.

The reformers would do well to read Federalist 10 so we may get on with the business of legislation.

ORRIN G. HATCH.

6

The Electoral College
Statement by Senator Daniel Patrick Moynihan
(D., N.Y.) on the
Floor of the United States Senate
Wednesday, June 27, 1979

Mr. Moynihan. Mr. President, I rise to speak briefly and for the first time in what I believe will be an extended debate on the matter before us, Senate Joint Resolution 28. I wish to address this subject in the context, as I see it, of the historical experience of the American Constitution and the American political system.

There is no fact more singular about our Constitution than its durability. As a written constitution, it is the oldest in the world save for the medieval Constitution of Iceland, which still persists in that small nation. No other large industrial, and certainly no continental, nation has anything like our experience of a sustained and stable government under a written constitution basically unchanged from its original construction.

We, perhaps, do not understand how singular this history is. If I may make a personal comment, I recall that one afternoon in the General Assembly Hall of the United Nations, in the course of a long debate on a not altogether absorbing subject, I found myself looking at the two large scoreboards, as one might say, located in the front of the Assembly Hall, on which the member nations are listed and where their votes are recorded.

I found myself asking how many of the 143 (now 151) nation members of the U.N. both had existed in 1914 and had not had their governments changed by force since 1914. It was not a great exercise to determine that in that great universe of nations, exactly seven met

151

both criteria, that they both existed in 1914 and had not had their form of government changed since.

There are some who might ascribe our good fortune to the insularity of the Nation in its early years, and the size and strength of the Nation in its later years. But I would say that in no small measure it has also been the result of the genius of the American Constitution and the way it has served this political community for almost two centuries.

I would not disguise, at the outset, my sense of the measure before the Senate today, proposing the abolition of the electoral college. In the guise of perfecting an alleged weakness in the Constitution, it in fact proposes the most radical transformation in our political system that has ever been considered, a transformation so radical and so ominous, in my view, as to require of this body the most solemn, prolonged and prayerful consideration. In particular, it requires a consideration that will reach back to our beginning, to learn how we built and how it came about that we built better than we knew. . . .

I would stress once again the idea the Founding Fathers had learned from history. They had studied its principles and judged that liberty was not just a quality characteristic of the ancient peoples from which the American peoples sprang, but was a principle of government of which any person who would learn enough natural science would persuade himself.

They recognized that republics in the past had been turbulent. They had all studied with great attention the history of Greece and of Rome. There had been democracies in both places—or republics if they were not democracies—which at certain times witnessed the appeal of one man or of one issue which came along and swept away the judgment of the people. And in the aftermath, what did they find but a ruined and defunct republic and a tyranny in its place?

So the Americans developed these new discoveries—as they saw them—separation of powers, the independent judiciary, the representation directly and indirectly of people and States in the Congress, a principle that involved not just one majority, but in the most important sense, many majorities.

Dr. Judith Best, the distinguished professor of political science at the State University of New York in Cortland, New York, and one of the foremost authorities on the electoral college, has spoken at length and with special clarity on the principle of concurrent majorities. In her testimony earlier this year before the Subcommittee on the Constitution, she put it quite luculently when she said, ". . . the principle of concurrent majority, is, has been, and was intended to be the American idea of democracy because the size of the popular vote is not sufficient to maintain liberty.''

All through our system we find majorities at work, but they have to be at work simultaneously. John C. Calhoun referred to them as concurrent majorities, and while he often spoke only of the States and the Federal Government, he perceived a self-evident property of our constitutional arrangements to be found everywhere. A concurrent majority is required between the House of Representatives, based upon the direct election of the people, and a majority in the U.S. Senate, Members of which at that time were indirectly elected through the State legislatures and which to this day represents the States and the people of the several States, regardless of their actual numbers. It is a majority of the States which counts in this body, not the majority of the population, *per se.*

Concurrent majorities are also required between sufficient majorities in both Houses of this Congress and the Presidency to enact a law, while the President himself comes to office by having achieved a majority of the electoral votes cast. The power subsequently evolved, but clearly anticipated by the framers—and I think this is settled—that the Supreme Court may review the acts of the Congress and the President in their concurrent majorities, and the majority of the court could judge upon constitutionality.

This pervasive and understood principle of the Constitution was thought to be—and who would argue that history has not supported that expectation—learned from history. And of all these majorities, none was more subtle or more central to their thinking than the majorities required to elect a President.

Again there would be several majorities, not in any rigid, absolute sense but in the sense that a clear preponderance of choice would emerge. The President would be elected by a majority of the popular vote and by a majority of the States. That has been our principle ever since. It is the principle enshrined in the electoral college, and it has been the basic institution which has given structure to American politics, and the politics of our Presidency.

At an early time in our history the electoral college changed its nature from a deliberative body which followed its own will, to a body which simply reflected the majority of the electors as they voted in their several States.

While we are a people very much given to the principle of written constitutional arrangements, I believe we have shown a capacity in our Government to adopt through practice matters which attain to the condition of principle. As an example, early in the Republic it became understood that a President would only serve two terms. George Washington established that. It was a century and a half before it was written into the Constitution. Yet it had the effect of a constitutional principle for all but the Administration of one President in a wartime situation, and that was very special indeed. Even so, that experience led to its being written down as an amendment to the Constitution itself. When, in fact, an informal constitutional principle was violated it soon became a formal one.

That tradition served us well for a very long period. It served us with respect to the single great problem which republics have always dealt with, which is how to persuade persons in power to leave power. It is a problem which, for example, the republics founded in Latin America in the early 19th century never successfully coped with, or rarely did. This led, in the Mexican Republic, for example, to an eventual recognition that no one ever left power of his own accord, resulting in a constitutional provision for only one term and one term only.

Our election of 1800 marked the most remarkable and most enduring of all political events in our history: the party out of power won an election and the party in power voluntarily left office. It was John Adams who was defeated when the votes finally came in from the South, and he went back to Quincy, Massachusetts, thinking himself a failure, having turned over the Treasury, the Great Seal, and the Army of the United States to Thomas Jefferson. Far from being a failure, he began democracy in the modern world.

He proved that it could work. It does not work everywhere. We are reduced, to this day, to some 35 democratic societies in the world, about the same number there were in 1914. But the oldest constitutional democracy is ours, and it lives under the Constitution established with great sensitivity for the need to see that power is never installed, save when it is consented to by more than one majority. That was the principle of the electoral college.

There is another aspect of our Constitution, one, I think, perhaps not always recognized that assumes conflict in political systems. This is not ordinary; this is unusual.

There is no prior constitution anywhere, even in the ancient constitutions of the Greeks, which recognized that conflict is normal to a political system and needs to be organized and channeled. A much more common assumption was that of monarchy, in which the king is assumed to represent the interests of all, and what the king does, is by definition, harmonious with the interests of all; or, consider the curious doctrine of the Soviets, which they acquire from Marx, that such are the basic harmonies of communist society that, after a period of socialism, that state will wither away, the state being coercive by nature and there being no need to coerce in a society where natural harmonies had been allowed to evolve.

James Madison knew better. He knew conflict is normal and perpetual. He also believed it could be controlled. And, of course, again, an extraconstitutional institution emerged, one which, interestingly, the founders had feared, but to which they very clearly lent their formidable energies and enterprise. The political party emerged. And from the beginning of the Republic, or to be more precise, from 1796, our third Presidential election, political parties developed for the purpose of organizing conflict and limiting conflict.

Only once have we seen them disappear in that brief period, in the 1820's. In the election of 1820, with the first appearance of the so-called faithless elector, Mr. Plummer of New Hampshire decided that only George Washington should be entitled to the honor of having been unanimously elected by the electoral college, and so cast his vote for John Quincy Adams. Even there, we see the electoral college being used as an institution to define majorities, and the parties that emerged had as their single most characteristic quality—again different from anything else in the experience of republics—that they were not ideological, that they were not sectional nor confessional, and rarely, in the two great parties, extremist.

It has been a source of frustration in the youth of as many generations as this Republic can measure that our parties have not been extremist. And if we look to the question, why have they not been this way, the answer is that the electoral college makes it impossible for them to be extremist if they are to continue effectively to be parties. Indeed, when some have begun to do so, they have ceased to exist.

The electoral college requires the assembly of consent—again, concurrent majorities—in one part of the country and another part of the country, and yet another part, all defined in terms of several States. It has as its extraordinary ability the formation of consensus as between widely differing regions, political purposes and styles, and political agendas. It has as its purpose and function the narrowing of differences, a narrowing which is repeatedly to be encountered in the narrow range of votes as between the parties in Presidential elections. There are few landslides as we call them.

And these landslides are really nothing of the sort. They rarely attain to 60 percent of the vote. When, in fact, one party momentarily belongs to an extreme faction it almost instantly is hugely rebuffed. It has been the experience of two centuries that just as instantly, they resort to a traditional practice of obtaining consensus, retaining a structure of concurrent majorities around the Nation that makes it possible to win a majority of the votes and electoral college, and thereafter, to govern with the legitimacy that has come of attaining to such diverse majorities.

Mr. President, I recapitulate, to state my judgment—and it can only be mine—that the proposal before us, in the guise of perfecting an alleged weakness in the Constitution, proposes the most radical transformation in our constitutional system that has ever been considered.

I remarked that the Founders devised our system with the idea of a network of concurrent majorities which would be required to exercise power. The fundamental thrust of this measure, however unintended— nonetheless it seems to be ineluctably clear—would be to abolish that principle of concurrent majority.

If there is once introduced into the Constitution the proposition that a President may routinely be elected by 40 percent of the vote, you have the most ironic of all outcomes, that in the name of majoritarianism we have abolished even that single majority which the Founders so feared.

Mr. President, politics is an argument about the future, and no one knows that future. However, as Hamilton and his colleagues argued, the study of history can give you some sense of probabilities. If we would study the modern history of Europe as they studied the ancient history of Greece, what would we repeatedly encounter but a democratic republican society succumbing to a plebiscitory majority, to one man, and to the end of the republic?

It happened in France; it happened in Italy; it happened in Germany. Almost the only places it has not happened in Europe on one occasion or another—I dare to suggest that it is an interesting point—are the constitutional monarchies.

Indeed, there was a moment, recently, when the only democracies left in Europe were constitutional monarchies. Having a hereditary chief of state, they never had to elect one with real power, and they could govern from their legislatures, where members were elected in individual constituencies as is the case in Britain today. They never succumbed to the ever-present threat of an overwhelming issue, an over-powering person, and the end of liberty. That is precisely what we invite if we adopt this radical measure.

Consider the situation: We shall have introduced the runoff, the very symbol of splintered European political systems, where no majority ever can be accumulated by the political process of one party presenting itself to the country and asking for a majority.

Why? Because it maintains its internal cohesion by the narrowness of its agenda, which is always and repeatedly reflected in the narrowness of its votes.

There are two ways to maintain a political party. Roughly speaking, there are two models.

On the one hand, one can assemble a narrow agenda of issues and find a constituency that cares strongly about those issues and will vote for one's party regardless, as long as it maintains that narrow agenda, that purity of doctrine, for that constituency will begin to dissolve when that purity begins to be diluted. That is the fate of democracies where it is not necessary to win a majority of the vote the first time out, and where it becomes possible to take the chance on winning a majority in the runoff.

The nature of the American political party which, as I said, has been the despair of every generation of college youth since John Quincy Adams, is that *it seeks a majority to begin with.* It is broad. It tends to dull conflict that is inspiring to youth and to seek much that is consoling to age, to wit, a not always pristine consensus.

What will we see if this resolution should come into law? To repeat, Mr. President, we do not know what we will see, but we know what others have encountered. We will see a situation in which at the very least we will have four parties because both of the major parties incorporates within themselves two parties.

One of the great influences of the electoral college is that after the party convention takes place the party that loses stays in the party, so to speak. Otherwise, there would be no prospect, even for the minimal rewards that go to the losing faction. But under this amendment, why not go off and run on your own?

Conceivably, at least four people will run. It will become normal. It would not be abnormal for fourteen. And you get a kind of randomness in outcome that is characteristic of a purposeless system. Anyone feeling strongly, as people will, and legitimately, about issues, will say: "What if I run and get 19 percent of the vote, and the next highest person gets 24 or 39, and together we go into the runoff, and who knows but that I will emerge?"

It will be a normal and legitimate calculation, and it will be a calculation that will have as its most distinguishing characteristic that no one would any longer think of those units of government, the States, which more and more, as we progress into the 20th century, become indispensable to the management of a governmental system which is increasingly loaded with tasks.

Theodore H. White, in a graphic description of events on election night as he would foresee them, suggests all the drama we know so well—as the early returns from Massachusetts, South Carolina, and Florida come in and then the great progression across the continent to California, Alaska and Hawaii begins—would dissipate. To the contrary, as the undifferentiated votes mounted up, the pressures would be on the mountain States and then the coastal States and the island State, to get out votes to change outcomes. There would be genuine pressures to fraud and abuse. It would be an election no one understood until the next day or the day after, with recounts that go on forever, and in any event, with no conclusion, and a runoff to come. The drama, the dignity, the decisiveness and finality of the American political system would be drained away in an endless sequence of contests, disputed outcomes, and more contests to resolve outcomes already disrupted.

That is how legitimacy is lost. That is how a nation trivializes those solemn events that make for the singlemost important ingredient of a civil society, which is trust. . . .

Mr. President, there is a solemn obligation of persons who have been blessed, as we have been blessed by a stable political system to look to that stability as the most precious inheritance anyone can have. Look about the world and think of the experience of mankind in this generation. Ask what society has lived from 1813 without foreign invasion. Ask what society has never known a break in its congressional or presidential or judicial successions. Ask what society so accepts the principles of the Constitution as to enable the Supreme Court, appointed for life, to strike down laws of this very legislature, and to do so with heightened respect when it fulfills its constitutional mandate.

Ask what the legitimacy of justice is once we tinker with the balancing phenomenon of the electoral college.

We have a republic. It has endured. We trifle with its arrangement at a risk not only to the future of that republic, but, most assuredly, to the reputation of this generation of political men and women. . . .

I hope the day does not come when tearing the Constitution asunder we effectively diminish the role of the President of the United States that as men or women are elected with so narrow a base that in order to continue in office—given the intensity of factions there that brought the person there in the first place, and the narrowness of base that threatens that incumbency—they commence to consider the most unpresidential and anti-republican of temptations.

We have prospered and endured. Let us hope that we shall continue to do so. There is work aplenty before this Congress. Let us get on with that work and leave the Constitution be. If the time comes when the true experience of an emergency arises because of the extraconstitutional practices that obtain as to the condition of principle, as was the case when the two-term practice was broken and Congress and the State legislatures therein did react, then the time to consider a measure such as this will be upon us. But let us wait until its necessity is plain.

Index

161

About the Author

Judith A. Best, distinguished teaching professor of political science at the State University of New York at Cortland, received her master's degree from the University of Michigan and Ph.D. from Cornell University. She is the author of *The Case Against Direct Election of the President* (Cornell University Press, 1975), *The Mainstream of Western Political Thought* (Human Sciences Press, 1980) and *National Representation for the District of Columbia* (University Publications of America, 1984), and is a member of the board of editors of *Presidential Studies Quarterly*. In 1977 she received the New York State University Chancellor's Award for Excellence in Teaching, and in 1986 was awarded the American Higher Education Association and the Carnegie Foundation Honor Salute for Education Leadership. At the request of the U.S. Senate Committee on the Judiciary, she has served on several occasions as an expert witness on the electoral college system.